Embattled Memories

Introduction

The Korean War Memories on It's Fiftieth Anniversary

The Korean War began in 1950 and ended in an armistice in 1953. More than six decades have passed since then. When I began my writings for this book in 2005, the Korean War memories had just passed their half-century anniversary, a substantial marker of the war's being subject to our memory construction for more than fifty years. The anniversaries of historical events often facilitate the introduction of new memory texts into public space. Because of its timing, the war's fiftieth anniversary in particular had the potential to provoke many actors to join in the process of constructing memories. Expectations were that survivors of both civilians and veterans, with a heightened sense of their limited life spans, might step forward to tell their untold stories to others. The fiftieth anniversary also provided the memory industry with legitimate and lucrative opportunities to market a historical event whose image is archaic, yet still relatively lucid in the minds of contemporary audiences. Political institutions also might be attentive to this heightened memory space where they can reiterate, articulate, and reaffirm the historical narrative in hegemony that resonates with societal norms and values.

The fiftieth anniversary of the Korean War thus offered memory scholars the unique opportunity to explore how memories are continuously reconstructed in a way that reflects the ongoing interactions between the past and the present. Likewise, the fiftieth anniversary has created a unique context in which one can critically peruse memories in action. While producing many cultural products that reinforce habitual frameworks of appreciating the war, the anniversary has interrupted the status quo of remembering with the influx of counter-memories as well as the reemergence of power relations in the memory process. Given this milieu, the aim of this book is to critically witness such memory constructions that have taken place recently within the context of the fiftieth anniversary of the Korean War.

thesis

More specifically, this book introduces five discrete memory sites in the United States and South Korea where counter-memories have recently clashed with official memories. The sites include U.S. media coverage of the No Gun Ri killings (1999–2001), female survivors' recollections of No Gun Ri (2005), the PBS documentary *Battle for Korea* (2001), the Utah Korean War Memorial (2003), and the statue of General Douglas MacArthur in South Korea (2005). I do not argue that these memory sites held more relevance than countless other Korean War memory sites that exist across the world. Nor do I intend to convince the reader that these sites are representative of the current dynamics of memory constructions regarding the Korean War. In fact, I did not seek out these memory sites on purpose. Rather, they serendipitously, inescapably, or even irresistibly came to my attention as I shifted my intellectual and personal journey from South Korea to the United States during the last decade. I encountered many of the memory agents and objects examined in this book at local memorial sites through which I have traveled or near which I have lived. The names of these sites are Youngdong, Daejeon, Nogunri, Incheon in South Korea, and Salt Lake City in the United States. Unlike national memorial sites, these local sites have offered not only sacrosanct zones where one can pause to contemplate meanings of historical events but also hybrid spaces where one can engage in mundane activities while being reminded of the relevance of past events. Thus, these local memorial sites have provided me with optimal ethnographic fields of memory studies where I could witness the acts of remembering in the most imminent, present context. I also have come to realize that it is the very specificity of provincial locations that has transformed an eclectic collection of memory sites into a meaningful memory collage communicating the notion that collective memories of the Korean War are *unsettling* at the current dynamic juncture of official memories and counter-memories of the war.

The process of writing this book has required me to engage in the very difficult task of translating meanings of words, images, and performance from one culture to the other. I have published this book in English with a university press in the United States. Yet many people whom I interviewed for this study speak only Korean. There also exist documents written only in Korean that became important references for this book. Given these factors, translation has become a critical part of my writing. Although my immersion in both South Korea and the United States has enabled me to identify equivalent signs for the same meaning in two different cultures, it also has provided me with a strong sense that meanings cannot easily travel through cross-cultural signs. Translation is beyond a technical process. It is thereby a daunting task to simultaneously, independently, and comparatively make sense of meanings in a cross-cultural context. I thus would like to remind readers of the possibilities of disjuncture and fracture that may have occurred in the process of translation. I am sure that much of the meaning that I intended to communicate can be found in what is said in this book. Yet I also would not overlook possible significant meanings that might not have survived in translation.

The book consists of five chapters, each of which explores a memory site of the Korean War. Chapter 1 examines how the U.S. media have both remembered and thereafter forgotten the incident in which U.S. troops killed South Korean civilians who were taking refuge on the trestles of the No Gun Ri Bridge at an early stage of the Korean War. Chapter 2 illuminates the way in which the female survivors—the primary witnesses of the No Gun Ri killings—have communicated their unutterable trauma through the Confucian script of motherhood. Chapter 3 investigates media's use of newly found archival images by examining the historical documentary film *Battle for Korea,* which portrays the Korean War by synthesizing archival films, some of which have never been investigated before. Chapter 4 goes on to look at the Utah Korean War Memorial that local veterans erected in 2003 at Memory Grove Park in Salt Lake City. This is a case study of a broader phenomenon of memorialization of the Korean War that has taken place in towns and cities across the United States since the fiftieth anniversary. The final and fifth chapter illuminates recent iconoclastic actions that have taken place surrounding the statue of General Douglas MacArthur at Incheon in South Korea. The study in this chapter focuses on an ironic relationship between signs and memories by exploring the roles of a statue during a time of transition.

While illustrating the specific utterances, features, and power dynamics that have emerged from each site, this book as a whole also addresses four critical theses that may help us to appreciate the current memory constructions of the Korean War. First, *counter-memories are increasingly at stake in remembering the war.* It is important to note that the recent surge of counter-memories of the Korean War has animated, to varying degrees, long-dormant sites of remembrance across time and space. Until recently, the official narrative of the Korean War—America's mission to save South Korea from a malicious communistic force—has been well preserved and maintained as both the U.S. and the South Korean mainstream discourses of the war. Today, these amnesic, ossified memories of the Korean War have been confronted by newly arising counter-memories that shed light on neglected aspects of the war, such as its local contexts, civilian perspectives, the losses of individual soldiers, communists' accounts, and cross-cultural tensions. The clash between official memories and counter-memories has taken various forms and energies, and thus has resulted in varying consequences. Moreover, while counter-memories have largely been sanitized by the rigidity of official memories in the United States, they seem to have been more caustic in the rapidly evolving landscape of collective memories in South Korea. With close readings of five memory sites, this book therefore explores how the introduction of counter-memories can be channeled, blocked, or reshaped by the given frameworks of official memories within a specific context of remembering the Korean War.

Second, *media have played a substantial role in the current reconstruction of the Korean War.* In fact, the book is attentive to the fact that the five memory sites that it addresses are respectively characterized by five discrete media: newspapers, survivors' bodies, archival films, a memorial, and a statue. Memory consists of form as well as content. The investigation of memory thereby requires two critical tasks. One is to unpack the content of memories by identifying both the stories themselves (what is remembered as well as what is forgotten) and the way certain stories get told (how they are legitimized, narrativized, and naturalized). The other equally important task is to examine how the specific forms of media influence the way in which certain stories are manifested, performed, and (re)constructed. A medium is not simply the mere facade of memory; rather, it is a tangible institution whose unique materiality and syntax can play substantial roles in reconstructing memories in specific ways. In fact, it is noted that a variety of media forms have complicated the very process of facilitating (or deterring) the recent introduction of counter-memories in the context of the fiftieth anniversary of the Korean War. While the potential of survivors' bodies as a vehicle for counter-memories is undermined by given ideological constraints, a statue—which is often deemed a reactionary sign for carrying the narrative in hegemony—has become a dissenting medium that effectively reveals yet again subversive memories of the Korean War. As an attempt to illuminate such complex roles of the media in memory construction, this book thus investigates how the specific semiotic features of each medium in five memory sites have tuned the intensity, intricacies, and even nuances of recent clashes between official and counter-memories of the Korean War.

Third, *cultivating critical questions is a much more urgent task than providing the "right" answers.* Under the influence of both positivistic historiography and conventional war narratives, the Korean War in mainstream discourse largely has been illustrated with questions regarding military strategies, tactics, heroic sagas, and geopolitics. Resisting such habitual frameworks of the Korean War, this book employs a set of critical questions that scholars of memory studies have developed for understanding the complex relationship between the present and the past. Among these questions are the following: Who have been the actors involved with constructing specific memories? In what contexts has memory construction taken place? How have power relations navigated the meaning-making process in such acts of remembering? What stories have been (de) selected to accommodate a certain narrative, ideology, identity in hegemony? What factors have transformed transient memory into intransient history? As indicated in these questions, scholars in memory studies have squarely and persistently asked readers in the present to critically ponder "the way things might have been" as opposed to "the way things were" in our appreciation of past events. Supported by such scholarship, this book not only attempts to subject the Korean War accounts to critical queries of memory studies but also intends to cultivate a nuanced, yet critical set of questions that will provoke us to look at the Korean War memories not as a closed historical event but as a continual memory process.

Lastly, *one can produce only a partial, incomplete, and therefore tentative account of Korean War memories.* Unfaithful to its title, which embraces the name of only one country, the Korean War was literally a cosmopolitan war. Besides the United States, the Soviet Union, China, and both North and South Korea, about twenty other countries under the flagship of the United Nations participated in the war by sending either their military units or medical support to the Korean Peninsula. One can imagine that each nation has constructed unique, diverging, or even conflicting narratives of the Korean War in the subsequent process of remembering this event. I have continued to sense the existence of multiple narratives of the Korean War in an international context. For example, a student from China whom I met in my classroom told me how she grew up with a heroic song that proudly remembers the bravery of Chinese soldiers during the Korean War. Then there was the taxi driver from Ethiopia who took me to the Salt Lake City airport and told me of his nostalgic feelings about the good old days of Ethiopia when that country could afford to send troops to help an unknown nation in Asia. Next was the Turkish scholar whom I ran into at an academic event and who hinted to me that a sense of resentment has emerged within Turkish memories of its government's decision to become involved in the Korean conflict. Of course, it would be naive to think that these voices respectively represent all the citizens of each nation. Perhaps no one can really grasp the complex web of memories that the Korean War has spun across time and space. Such an unfathomable complexity, however, does not have to be a daunting omen for one who studies memories; rather it may act to rightfully encourage us to recognize that our acts of remembering can harvest only partial, incomplete, and thus tentative accounts of this past event. Certainly, the aim of this book is to produce not a comprehensive account but rather a hermeneutic text that invites more conversations regarding the Korean War.

concerning interpretation

CHAPTER 1

"Silencing" Memories

Why Are We Again Forgetting the No Gun Ri Story?

On September 29, 1999, with the comment "It was a story no one wanted to hear," the Associated Press (AP) brought an uneasy flashback of the Korean War to the American public's mind. Along with an in-depth analysis of declassified military records, the AP had interviewed dozens of Korean War veterans and No Gun Ri survivors by telephone and in person.[1] The long-submerged memories that had lasted nearly a human life span were fatigued, splintery, and malleable to reconstruction. Rather than claiming demonstrative truth, the Associated Press cautiously unfolded a horrific scene from a long-forgotten war: "American veterans of the Korean War say that in late July 1950, in the conflict's first desperate weeks, U.S. troops killed a large number of South Korean refugees, many of them women and children, trapped beneath a bridge at a hamlet called No Gun Ri. . . . What then happened under the concrete bridge cannot be reconstructed in full detail."[2]

The next day, the AP's account of the No Gun Ri incident appeared across the U.S. media, with many newspapers carrying an abbreviated

The No Gun Ri Bridge (2005)

version. Prestigious newspapers, including the *New York Times* and the *Washington Post,* gave special attention to the story by devoting a portion of their front pages to it. The *New York Times* published a picture of an elderly Asian woman standing in front of a bridge with a sullen expression, making a somewhat intense gesture. The caption ran: "Chun Choon Ja, a survivor, during a commemoration last year at the bridge near No Gun Ri." This enigmatic image of a Korean woman conjured the disturbing scene that had been forgotten for five decades. Considering the passage of time, the report was somewhat terse, and thus immediately raised a chain of questions: Why were we hearing the story now? How had the AP found this forgotten story? What caused such a tragic incident? How could we possibly know the details of incidents that took place five decades ago?

This special AP report was initiated by testimonies of the No Gun Ri survivors who had held on to their memories for those five decades. Under the authoritarian rule of the U.S.-allied South Korean government, however, survivors and victims' relatives were afraid to share their traumatic stories because they might be accused of being communist sympathizers. Nevertheless, Chung Eun-Yong, who lost his five-year-old son, Goo-Phil, and two-year-old daughter, Goo-Hi, had devoted his life to bringing public attention to this forgotten episode. He had collected all available archives related to the incident and in 1994 published a novel titled *Do You Know Our Pain?*[3] and based on the story told by the survivors. Moreover, he had sent petitions seeking compensation for the survivors and the victims' families to both the U.S. and the Korean governments. Even so, Chung's family and the No Gun Ri villagers found it difficult to find a media outlet; their files were rejected by both the South Korean and the U.S. governments. In the 1990s, when South Korea began to have a liberalized political atmosphere, a few Korean media reported the No Gun Ri incident, but it had little impact on the public's consciousness at that time.[4] This event did not receive international recognition until investigative reporters from the Associated Press brought it to the American public in 1999.

Many newspaper articles drew an analogy between the No Gun Ri incident and the 1969 My Lai massacre during the Vietnam War.[5] Both were U.S. atrocities involving foreign civilians; both would be "hard-sell" stories in the U.S. media.[6] In an intriguing difference, however, My Lai was told through pictures, whereas No Gun Ri was recalled through oral testimonies. The report of the My Lai massacre appeared with an emotion-provoking image that depicted the dead bodies of children and women,[7] whereas the coverage of the No Gun Ri incident had no similar eyewitness photo that could play "the primary role of convincing disbelieving publics about the atrocities."[8] Although the bullet-riddled bridge and the survivors' wounded bodies provocatively evoked tragic memories, they became visual evidence only when supported by verbal testimony. The backbone of the story thus became the testimony emerging from numerous memory sites, including official archives, evidence collected at the scene, the faltering voices of GIs,[9] and survivors' memories etched in their wounded bodies and minds.

Such eclectic utterances substantially validated the No Gun Ri story to the point that the AP investigative reporters—Sang-Hun Choe, Charles Hanley, Martha Mendoza, and Randy Herschaft—won two of journalism's most prestigious awards in 1999 and 2000: the Pulitzer Prize for investigative reporting and the George Polk Award for international reporting. Furthermore, influential media institutions' competitive coverage, along with substantial evidence, provoked the Pentagon to order an official investigation of the incident. After one year, however, Secretary of Defense William Cohen announced that a "thorough and exhaustive review"[10] by the U.S. Army was not able to uncover what had really occurred at No Gun Ri. Neither specific casualty figures nor the existence of orders to shoot could be clarified by their inquiry. Confirming the army's account, the Clinton administration, while officially acknowledging the American troops' killing of the innocent civilians, nevertheless called for a didactic closure by suggesting how the incident should be remembered: "As we honor those civilians who fell victim to this conflict, let us not forget that pain is not the only legacy of the Korean War. American and Korean veterans fought shoulder to shoulder in the harshest of conditions for the cause of freedom, and they prevailed. The vibrancy of democracy in the Republic of Korea, the strong alliance between our two peoples today is a testament to the sacrifices made by both of our nations 50 years ago."[11]

The official closure of the No Gun Ri investigation asked ex-GIs to bury their traumatic memories under the shining narrative of a noble mission while encouraging victims to ease their bitterness through gratitude for their country's prosperity. The U.S. government decided not to give a formal apology to the South Korean people, nor would it offer financial compensation to the victims' families. In fact, Clinton's statement used the word "regret," as opposed to "apology," a choice that provoked great resistance among South Korean survivors and victims' relatives.

We know that word choice shapes power relations in symbolic interaction. As Erving Goffman puts it, "apology" invites the offended party to say whether the "remedial message" has been received or is sufficient.[12] Through the word "regret," however, Clinton's statement diminished survivors' potential role in responding to an "apology." In fact, South Korean survivors' calling the U.S. Army report a "whitewash" became a faint echo that barely resonated with the public. After the U.S. media closed the No Gun Ri story, the British Broadcasting Corporation produced a compelling documentary, *Kill 'Em All* (2001), that showed how the official U.S. investigation may have manipulated testimonies and archives to gloss over facts about the incident. On April 14, 2007, six years after Clinton's statement, the Associated Press again revealed that during the 2001 investigation the U.S. Army dismissed a letter from the U.S. ambassador in

South Korea in 1950 that proved that the U.S. military had a policy of shooting approaching refugees during the Korean War. Nonetheless, this counter-voice did not last long in the U.S. media. The evidence of the No Gun Ri story quickly melted into the amnesia that is the American collective memory of the Korean War.

The purpose of my research is to analyze this trajectory of the No Gun Ri story from forgetting to remembering to forgetting again. This research has not attempted to draw detailed pictures of what really happened at No Gun Ri at the end of July 1950, a task that I believe to be impossible. Neither does it look at how meticulously the media have portrayed the incident. My research has not focused on "truth claims" themselves, but rather on narratives that are "the grammar of truth claims." This approach came from the realization that the media's constructed narratives often appear as accounts of "what the event actually was" as opposed to "what it might be." The media's accounts, often with no reflexivity, can easily create a situation that discourages the public from being critical appreciators of historical texts. Thus, this analysis of media texts could be completed only when it was accompanied by a comparative study of both texts: those onstage (the media texts) and those backstage (the primary sources). This realization encouraged me to look into survivors' accounts—the critical sources "standing" backstage behind the media texts of the No Gun Ri incident.

To get an account of survivors' testimonies and to compare them with the narratives in the media coverage, I conducted oral history interviews with twelve survivors and victims' relatives during the summer of 2005 at three sites in South Korea: Youngdong County, Taejeon City, and Seoul. The narrators[13] were selected because their testimonies were the primary ones used in the U.S. media coverage of the incident. The techniques of the oral history interview have developed among oral historians as a means of allowing voiceless people to tell their stories in their own words. Barbara Allen, an oral historian, points out that the terms "researcher" and "narrator" are more appropriately used in connection with the oral history interview, as opposed to the terms "interviewer" and "interviewee," which connote "doer" and "doee."[14] Taking Allen's suggestion, I refer to myself as the "researcher" and to the survivors and victims' relatives of the No Gun Ri incident as the "narrators" throughout this essay.

Although I met narrators more than five decades after the incident and after the U.S. Army had ended its investigation, their emotions had persisted so strongly that they vividly shared their memories. Even now, the bridge under which U.S. soldiers attacked these civilians functions as a viaduct of the railroad system. The bridge's presence, with its many bullet holes, has served as a mnemonic object, continuously inviting villagers to share their memories. Moreover, many of the survivors and victims' relatives still live in the same or nearby villages. Within this geographical cluster in rural South Korea, a relatively strong kinship remains that contributes to the maintenance of a solid collective memory. Survivors' memories allowed me not only to showcase the subversive attributes of survivors' testimonies in reconstructing a past event, but also to deepen my dissection of media texts by revealing the ways in which the media selectively highlighted as well as ignored survivors' testimonies in the process of forming narratives.

NARRATIVIZING, HEGEMONY, AND COLLECTIVE AMNESIA

Memory scholars have recognized collective memory as an active site where heterogeneous meanings, identities, and powers compete for hegemony. Memory studies have developed by identifying as well as analyzing varying degrees of discrete tensions that arise in memory construction, including tension between collective and individual memories, official (national) and vernacular (local) memories, images and words, written memories and oral testimonies, and ultimately the past and the present.[15] Tensions arising in memory construction invite struggling, negotiation, and ultimately manufacturing of an illusory consensus, what Gramsci calls the state of hegemony.[16]

Consensus in memory construction appears as a set of narratives. Maurice Halbwachs notes that the act of remembering is inevitably tamed by our "habit of recalling them [past events] in organized sets."[17] Past events are perceived as narratives that memory continuously remolds. Using a compelling metaphor, David Lowenthal suggests that our country (the present) has attempted to colonize the foreign country (the past) by reorganizing its events with contrived narratives. It is narrativizing that transforms the past events (mysterious, anomalous, and constantly changing texts) into the perceived events (palpable, shaped, and static texts).

Furthermore, narratives are functional devices through which past events are efficiently politicized to accommodate power relations in the present.[18] As John Bodnar notes, narratives are not merely "structures of meaning" but also "structures of power,"[19] whose formations skillfully navigate the act of remembering, a process of generating *the* narrative in hegemony as opposed to a narrative among many.

Narrativizing in collective memory is unique because it takes place in two domains—forgetting and remembering—both of which take place simultaneously as "co-constitutive processes."[20] Narratives are often constructed in such a way as to naturalize the arbitrary selection of memories: what to forget and what to remember. Forgetting is an indispensable act to the creation of hegemony, because it is used to exclude counter-evidences whose very presence contests narratives that have been shaped by the reigning power relation. Such a willful forgetfulness in the act of remembering has been called by different names: concerted forgetting, organized oblivion, and collective amnesia.[21]

Collective amnesia is particularly germane to war. Wars in American collective memory are remembered in terms of the rhetoric of heroism, stories that cherish the virtues of intrepidity, progress, and victory.[22] Within the narrative of triumph, military activities are often romanticized as patriotic, altruistic, and purely self-determined actions. Inhumanity does not appear as an inherent characteristic of war, but is considered as either the evidence of the enemy's immorality or an anecdotal tragedy that asks to be forgotten.

More than any other, the Korean War is exemplary in that its theme is largely shaped by the act of forgetting. Its official narrative—America's mission of saving South Korea from merciless Communist aggression—has maintained an absolute hegemonic power through forgetting a substantial body of counter-memories that historians and journalists have cultivated since the war broke out. One such counter-memory is the depiction of South Korean police atrocities toward civilians.[23] Another counter-memory is offered by historians who resist the reductive views of the war's cause by arguing that although international power relations aggravated the conflicts on the Korean Peninsula, the fundamental cause of the war resided within the local context of class conflicts resulting from Japanese colonialism.[24]

A more thorny issue among historians is America's role on the Korean Peninsula before and during the war. In 1945, when the Japanese colonial power withdrew from the peninsula, the Soviet Union and the United States, the winners of World War II, divided the Korean Peninsula along the 38th parallel and began to take on separate trusteeship of North Korea and South Korea. A number of historians have offered critiques suggesting that U.S. trustees increased domestic tension by accusing many Korean citizens of being Communist sympathizers. Ironically, the U.S. trusteeship, whose objective was to secure an ultimate liberation of South Korea, blocked many legitimate voices and actions that aspired to extirpate the legacy of Japanese colonial rule.[25] Worse, U.S. trusteeship favored conservative groups of landlords and businessmen, and even restored power to some former officers who persecuted their own fellow citizens during Japanese occupation. As Carter Eckert and his associates put it, "Unfortunately, what seemed middle-class and democratic by American standards was more often than not upper class, reactionary, and collaborationist by Korean standards in 1945."[26]

These counter-arguments, put forth by historians and news correspondents, seldom have entered American public memory of the Korean War. Public memory does not often contest the official narrative of the war: Communist atrocities as the cause and the valor of America's efforts to rescue an endangered Korean Peninsula as the response. This narrative always has been manifested in U.S. public memory as a dogmatic truth, but never appeared as one of many plausible, yet unconfirmed narratives. As Paul Pierpaoli puts it, the rigid mentality of 1950s McCarthyism highly politicized the Korean War "in a most peculiar and destructive way."[27]

In this barren landscape of Korean War memory, the U.S. media's introduction of the No Gun Ri incident—atrocities by American soldiers— seemed to shock historians, since "there was no previous report of any atrocity of this magnitude by United States forces in the Korean War."[28] The abrupt emergence of the No Gun Ri accounts in the U.S. media at the end of the 1990s may have reflected the evolving contexts of the memory of the war: the end of the Cold War era, the newly unearthed archives from the former Soviet bloc, and the end of these witnesses' life spans. In fact, many Korean War veterans' voices have been introduced recently in books such as *I Remember Korea* (2003) and *Voices from the Korean War*

(2004). It is important to examine whether these newly unearthed memories have functioned to trigger counter-narratives or to reinforce official narratives. As a critical witness of the evolving milieu of the Korean War, my research identifies four narratives emerging from the No Gun Ri text and examines whether each narrative enhances or counters the official account of the Korean War. Narrative themes that emerge from the various texts include: *Ill-equipped troops' unfortunate mistake* and *Fear-stricken soldiers' defensive action* from the media text; and *Two aliens in cross-cultural war* and *Salvation by hospitable communists* from the survivors' testimonies. In the following section, I will discuss the implications of each narrative within the larger context of U.S. memories of the Korean War, a process that will unveil both the political function of narrativizing as well as the intricate mechanism of forgetfulness in the act of remembering.

MEDIA NARRATIVE 1: ILL-EQUIPPED TROOPS' UNFORTUNATE MISTAKE

The story of No Gun Ri is particularly disturbing because most of the victims were women, children, and old men. It was not surprising that the media's greatest effort initially was devoted to finding a plausible answer to the uneasy question of why American soldiers on a saving mission had become involved in such a horrific action. Interestingly, within a few days, newspapers seemed to reach a solid consensus that the incident took place because the military was ill-trained and ill-equipped during the early stages of the war. Many articles emphasized the fact that the soldiers at No Gun Ri were green recruits from the U.S. occupation of Tokyo; they were teenage soldiers plucked out of Japan and dropped into the front lines of the war without proper training. In brief, the No Gun Ri incident is described as "ill-equipped troops' unfortunate mistake."

Soon the Pentagon briefing prompted by the AP report validated this narrative. It stressed that American troops during the war were in bad shape "because of the large reduction in resources available to the military for training and equipment following World War II."[29] The officials' emphasis on the poor condition of troops straddled a fine line between ascribing the killing of civilians to the troops' poor training and justifying the incident as an inevitable by-product of a dangerous situation.

Although newspapers, following the official voice, collectively published the "ill-equipped troops" narrative as factual information, they made few efforts to look into the complex picture of unready troops thrown onto the battlefield. In their memoirs, the veterans consistently reported that they faced chaos in the first stage of the war, not only because they were not equipped with competitive and abundant weapons, but also because they were hardly aware of the cause of the conflict; such knowledge would have acted to strengthen their morale. In her book *War in Korea*, Marguerite Higgins, who witnessed the Korean War as a correspondent for the *New York Herald Tribune*, reported, "If, by the end of August, you asked any front-line GI what he was fighting for, he felt—because most GIs aren't very articulate—just as embarrassed at the question as he had been three months before."[30] The confusion appears to have soared among American soldiers and the public to the point that it forced President Truman to make a special report to the nation to address why American troops had to be deployed to such a far-off country: "These men of ours are engaged once more in the age-old struggle for human liberty. Our men, and the men of other free nations, are defending with their lives the cause of freedom in the world. They are fighting for the proposition that peace shall be the law of this earth."[31] Truman's adamant voice confirming the war's cause with abstract concepts did not respond directly to the veterans' confusion from the battlefield. Five decades later, the media's narrative of an ill-equipped army still could not embrace the complex backdrop of the No Gun Ri incident, at which U.S. soldiers had suffered from a lack of morale as well as insufficient weaponry. Worse, the narrative of "ill-equipped troops' unfortunate mistake" was taken as a call for better preparation for another war rather than a warning about the inhumane characteristics of war.

As a result, the tone of the media's voice became identical to that of the official voice, demonstrating a strong tendency to locate this tragic episode within a framework of lessons for future wars. Through this refracted lens, a destructive war appeared as an essential human activity that with better preparation could have been transformed into a positive experience. As an exemplary case, an editorial in the *Boston Globe* titled "Casualties of an Unready Army" opined: "The US military's job is to fight wars skillfully and as humanely as possible. The Defense Department should make a full accounting of what happened at No Gun Ri and teach new generations of soldiers to be ready to wage war honorably."[32] Narrativizing No Gun Ri as a lesson for a better kind of war seemed to have culminated in President Clinton's address at Arlington National Cemetery on November 11, 1999. Echoing the No Gun Ri narrative, he emphasized that a new military spending bill would assure "the best-trained, best-equipped, best-prepared" military in the world.[33] Such an official voice endorses the hegemonic process of generating *the* narrative as opposed to *a* narrative among many in remembering the Korean War. With official endorsement, the "ill-equipped troops' unfortunate mistake" narrative has framed the No Gun Ri story as an anecdotal war tragedy that can be allowed to fall into the domain of forgetfulness. Moreover, the narrative successfully displaces the many counter-evidences, the very presence of which would contest official narratives of the Korean War. After No Gun Ri, South Koreans filed more than sixty cases of atrocities allegedly committed by the U.S. Army during the war. No episode, however, has gotten as much attention from the U.S. public as No Gun Ri. The hegemonic narrative, "Ill-equipped troops' unfortunate mistake," has left little room for a possible counter-narrative: "No Gun Ri could be one of many."

MEDIA NARRATIVE 2: FEAR-STRICKEN SOLDIERS'
DEFENSIVE ACTION

The second narrative collectively formed in U.S. newspaper coverage was the fear of Communist infiltration among American soldiers during the war. Most newspapers repeatedly mentioned that American soldiers panicked over the possibility that North Korean Communists were hiding among refugee groups. This narrative echoes one of the most stark aspects of the battlefield reality: the U.S. Army experienced tremendous difficulty in distinguishing friends (refugees) from foes (infiltrators), and this confusion increased the rate of casualties. In the media coverage, this army-inspired account appeared along with a speculative statement that the GIs' killing of civilians could have been a defensive action aimed at infiltrated foes hiding among refugee groups beneath the bridge.

However, it is critical to note that the narrative of fear formed by the media neglected the fact that "legitimate fear" provoked on a chaotic battlefield inevitably created another "legitimate fear" among other actors.

The soldiers' fear of potential infiltrators in turn engendered fear among Korean civilians that they could be killed without discretion. In fact, the AP investigative team found that the U.S. Army's decision to shoot civilians took place more systematically than the fear narrative suggests. Investigating the incident, the AP uncovered declassified U.S. Air Force reports showing that pilots deliberately attacked "people in white" who were suspected to harbor disguised North Koreans.[34]

As further suggestive evidence in the No Gun Ri incident, the AP also released two significant documents found in the U.S. National Archives. The first one, dated July 27, 1950, was a signed order from General William B. Kean to his 25th Infantry Division: "All civilians seen in this area are to be considered as enemy and action taken accordingly." The second was a communication log from the First Cavalry's Eighth Regiment that was recorded just two days before the incident at No Gun Ri: "No refugees to cross the front line. Fire everyone trying to cross lines. Use discretion in case of women and children."[35] These official documents, surfacing half a century after the war, imply that civilians were in an extremely vulnerable position. It is possible that the "people in white" often targeted by the U.S. Air Force could have been North Korean infiltrators, but there is a far greater likelihood that they were merely civilian refugees, since white clothing was the most common attire among ordinary Koreans at that time. White clothing was also an emblem of the Korean national identity. On his field trip to Korea in the summer of 1947, American anthropologist Cornelius Osgood found that white clothing was one of the strongest Korean traditions—not even the Japanese occupiers could alter it. He reported: "A word must be said about the color of the Korean costume. Basically it is white for all sexes, seasons, and ages.... The Japanese managed to insinuate their machine-made cotton yard goods until today the home manufacture of cloth has been greatly reduced. The conquerors' last attempt toward change was the introduction of black socks, but these the Koreans resisted. Black is a color to wear on the head; on their feet they still wear white."[36]

Neither ordinariness nor the national connotation of white clothing among Koreans was recognized in the process of forming the "fear-stricken soldiers' defensive action" narrative. Saturating the situation with a sense of fear among U.S. soldiers alone, the narrative left "people in white" as unidentified, clandestine, and thus fear-provoking groups.

In this guerrilla-type battlefield, neither soldiers nor civilians could secure their own safety, no matter where they were. Neither soldiers nor civilians could free themselves from this notion of the fear of being killed. The soldiers had a means of defense, but the civilians had none. In a 2005 article in *Diplomatic History*, Sahr Conway-Lanz pointed out that No Gun Ri should be understood within a larger context of the war where the U.S. military problematically handled civilian refugees. He wrote that during the early stages of the Korean War, "American soldiers had developed a tendency to regard all Korean civilians near the battle zone as the enemy."[37] In the American collective memory of the war, however, this vulnerable battlefield seems to be witnessed and recalled mainly through the fear from soldiers' eyes or through the strategic lenses of the army. In the media's No Gun Ri account, while veterans are vocal in elaborating their fears, survivors' testimonies are rarely used to illustrate their "legitimate fears." Furthermore, survivors of the incident were hardly allowed in media coverage to make their claims that there was no North Korean infiltration. This continuous silencing of the civilians' voice is the most noticeable aspect found in the media's account of the No Gun Ri story.

SURVIVORS AS SUPPORTING WITNESSES

One of the first pieces of information that I learned in my fieldwork in South Korea was that most victims of the incident were not No Gun Ri villagers, but rather refugees from both Chu Gok Ri and Im Ke Ri in Youngdong County who were fleeing to the South to escape from the advancing North Korean troops. Youngdong County has been well known as the village of the royal Chungs (Young-Il) family, a Yangban[38] clan whose ancestors were noted scholars in the Choson Dynasty, a hierarchical Confucian kingdom. Thus, many victims of the No Gun Ri incident have the family name Chung.

In interviews with the author, each narrator displayed distinctive characteristics in claiming his or her own traumas as well as the veracity of his or her testimony. All of them, however, collectively projected how the incident had destroyed not only their physical bodies but also their relationships with loved ones. These survivors' individual stories assert that the statistical reports of civilian casualties of war in official historical accounts make sense to the public only when accompanied by individual accounts of how war devastates actual lives. Yet few articles in the U.S. media introduced any survivor's memory as an individual account, rich with its complex, layered, and distinguished life story. Rather, most articles selected parts of survivors' testimonies and merely inserted them into a tapestry-like account, weaving together many discrete voices from GIs' testimonies, editorial notes, experts' comments, and written documents.

Moreover, in the media's narrative construction, survivors' testimonies were not appraised as independent testimonies that were valued in and of themselves. Rather, it was the GIs' testimonies that substantiated as well as corroborated memories from survivors and from victims' relatives. For instance, on September 30, 1999, when the news broke about the No Gun Ri incident, newspapers used headlines and subheads that emphasized the significance of the veterans' voices as confirmers of the survivors' testimonies. They included such titles as "G.I.'s Tell of a U.S. Massacre in Korean War," "Ex-soldiers Confirm Villagers' Accounts," and "Vets Back S. Koreans' Claim that GIs Massacred Civilians."[39] As supporting witnesses, survivors' testimonies were used largely to evoke abstract feelings of trauma and horror rather than to enhance readers' understanding. For instance, the following types of survivors' testimonies were repeatedly cited in the U.S. media: "the American soldiers played with our lives like boys playing with fire"[40] and "people pulled dead bodies around them for protection."[41]

By treating survivors as supporting witnesses, the U.S. media obscured some critical narratives embedded in the survivors' memories. For instance, when I interviewed narrators, I noticed that most survivors began their stories not from the day of air strafing or machine-gunning under the tunnel, but from the days of refuge in the mountains at Im Ke Ri. Unlike the media account, survivors' testimonies recognized a series of episodes before and after the No Gun Ri tunnel as constituting a full account of the incident. The following is an outline of the composite story found in the survivors' testimonies:

1. Evacuation from villages
2. Taking refuge in mountains at Im Ke Ri
3. Being rousted by American soldiers
4. Climbing down (voluntarily) from mountains
5. Staying the night in open air (near the base of U.S. troops)

6. Being inspected by American soldiers on railroad
7. Abrupt air strafing on railroad
8. Scrambling (voluntarily or by force) into No Gun Ri tunnel
9. Being attacked by the U.S. soldiers for three nights under the bridge
10. Saved by North Korean soldiers
11. Afterward, telling their life stories

Interestingly, no survivor could recollect thoroughly all of these episodes. For different reasons, some kept clearer images of certain parts than of others. Some could recollect only discrete images and sounds without making a full story. Nevertheless, it was clear that their recollections took place in terms of all of the episodes, whether recalled in a linear or nonlinear manner. From a thread of testimonies, however, the official lenses of the No Gun Ri incident tend to isolate two episodes: the air strafing on the railroad and the machine-gunning in the tunnel. As a result, many countermemories embraced in the contextual background before and after the two episodes were not recognized in the media's construction of the narratives.

For example, in the formation of the "fear-stricken soldiers' defensive action" narrative, many U.S. newspapers introduced GIs' testimonies that they witnessed the North Korean soldiers infiltrating refugee groups. Yet the GIs' claim of a North Korean presence could be countered by many detailed episodes found among the survivors' testimonies such as "the refugees had been rousted by U.S. soldiers from nearby villages," "refugees who tended to trust U.S. soldiers climbed down the mountain," "refugees' luggage was inspected by American soldiers on the railroad (only household utensils were taken away)," and "refugees in the tunnel were scouted by American soldiers during the first day." Such survivors' claims dispute the speculation that the refugee group at No Gun Ri was suspicious or threatening enough to provoke defensive violence. To elaborate this point, I will discuss two narratives taken from survivors' testimonies whose themes, angles, and even tone are quite different from those of dominant media narratives.

SURVIVORS' NARRATIVE 1: TWO ALIENS IN CROSS-CULTURAL WAR

Many survivors and victims' relatives claimed that it was the issue of race that made it possible for humans to perform such cruel acts toward other humans. Chung Koo-Hun said, "I believe the incident was a massacre based on racial discrimination. If they were considering us as valuable as at least livestock, they wouldn't have killed us in such a brutal way." Park Sun-Yong, who witnessed the deaths of her two babies, also argued that "American soldiers must have considered us no better than scum, otherwise they could not have undertaken such cruelty as killing those poor babies." In fact, both survivors' testimonies and journalists' eyewitness accounts demonstrate that there had been tension between Korean civilians and American soldiers since their first encounter in 1945. Most Koreans in rural areas rarely had seen foreigners from the Western world. Chun Choon-Ja recalled, "I was scared just by looking at Americans. Their faces looked so different from us. We could not even communicate with them."

From the American soldiers' perspectives, the first encounters with Koreans also seem to have been tense. In the 1950s, Korea was little known to Westerners; thus the GIs knew little about Korea and its people before the war. Unlike Japan, Korea had been reluctant for a long time to open its nation to Western traders. When American soldiers landed on the Korean Peninsula in the 1950s, they seemed to be shocked at the sharp contrast between the modern images of Japan with its Western civilization and the indigenous scenes of Korea with its legacy of an isolated kingdom. During the war, Western correspondents witnessed that GIs frequently used the derogatory term "gook" in general reference to the Korean population.[42]

In addition to feelings of oddity in a strange land, American soldiers also had to cope with their inability to communicate with civilians, as related in survivors' testimonies. When faced with danger, many survivors begged American soldiers for their lives by telling them that they were just civilians. Park Sun-Yong recalled that when American soldiers scouted the tunnel, several refugees, including her nephew, who was majoring in English literature at Yonhee University, came out to meet them and tried to communicate with them. She said, "My nephew spoke English to them, but the rest of us, *regardless of whether they understood or not* [emphasis added], cried out in Korean: 'We are not communists! Please save our lives! We are innocent!'" Keum Cho-Ja, who knew a little Japanese language from living in Japan, tried to speak Japanese to the American soldiers tending to her wounds. She said, "I heard that Americans would understand Japanese. So, I asked them 'give me water' in Japanese. They *seemed* to think that I would die if I drank water. They kept saying to me 'No, no.'" Chung Koo-Ho recalled a brief conversation with American soldiers when they inspected refugees' luggage on the railroad. "I thought they would understand Japanese," he said. "So I told them 'save us' in Japanese. They looked at me for a while . . . and responded with the Japanese word for 'poor.'" Most survivors remembered the moment when they desperately attempted to communicate with American soldiers as they were on the verge of being killed. They rarely used English. Sometimes they spoke a little Japanese learned during the colonial period. Most times, however, they used Korean with intense body language, which barely made sense to the Americans. In any case, survivors seemed to have had a strong hope that their desperate messages could penetrate the foreign soldiers' minds.

The reality of the battlefield, however, seemed to be far from what the survivors expected. The following report from John Osborne, a correspondent for *Time* and *Life* magazines, implies a hopeless incommunicability that existed between the American soldiers and the Korean civilians during the war: "We occupied it [South Korea] for nearly three years and in this time we should have accumulated a considerable staff of military and civilian officials who came to know the country, the people, the language. It is true that many of the American civilian officials who were stationed in Korea before the war are there now. But I saw none of them at work in the field."[43]

When forming the *ill-equipped troops' unfortunate mistake* narrative, the U.S. media pointed to the lack of training and poor equipment as proof of being unprepared for war. Yet few articles mentioned the issue of language in this cross-cultural war. None pointed out that the inability to communicate with civilians in a guerrilla war not only made military operations ineffective, but also increased civilian casualties. In brief, although survivors' voices in the No Gun Ri incident ask us to ponder the possibility that racial attributes—different looks, cultures, and languages—can aggravate the inhumanity of war, the unique tensions in this cross-cultural war were not examined in U.S. media coverage.

SURVIVORS' NARRATIVE 2: SALVATION BY
HOSPITABLE COMMUNISTS

In the survivors' testimonies, the last day at the No Gun Ri tunnel evoked the day that American soldiers liberated the concentration camps during

World War II. On July 29, 1950, when U.S. troops pulled back from the area of No Gun Ri, survivors found themselves surrounded by a mysterious tranquillity. No more American soldiers were on the hills with guns aimed inside the tunnel. There was not even the sound of shooting. In the afternoon of that mysterious day, survivors were visited by North Korean soldiers, who offered their sorrow and indignation over the wretched scene in the tunnel. This was the most ironic moment of the No Gun Ri incident: refugees fleeing from a North Korean advance were liberated by the very troops from whom they were fleeing. North Korean soldiers, whom one of the survivors recalled as "soldiers with the same faces as us," became the first witnesses of the incident. In fact, tracking survivors' testimonies, Chung Koo-Do, a representative of the Committee for Unveiling Truth about the No Gun Ri Massacre, discovered an article in *Cho Sun In Min Bo*,[44] a progressive Korean newspaper, from August 19, 1950, that contained North Korean soldiers' accounts.

In interviews, several narrators testified that they were deeply moved by the generosity of the North Korean soldiers, who not only extricated them from the tunnel and showed them a safe path home, but also fed them. Yang Hae-Suk recalled, "Frankly, North Korean soldiers were our enemy at that time. They started the commotion. However, if they did not come to No Gun Ri . . . if American soldiers stayed there longer, no one would have survived from that tunnel." Chung Koo-Ho also remembered that the North Koreans had advised them not to leave the tunnel until nighttime; otherwise they would be killed by American air bombing. He said, "On the way home, North Korean soldiers even gave us meals. . . . I felt a sense of same race-consciousness." Such stories about the North Korean soldiers were completely missing from U.S. media coverage. In contrast to its vivid images embedded in oral memory, the last day at the bridge remained obscure in the official, institutional memory of the No Gun Ri incident.

One might argue that the story of the North Korean soldiers is not an episode necessary for reconstructing the account. Yet it is important to note that the question of how some refugees could survive under harsh attacks has continuously arisen. Plausible answers to this question were found among the survivors' testimonies, which recounted how they covered themselves with dead bodies or how their parents sacrificed their own bodies to provide protection for their children. The gracious faces of the enemy soldiers, who in fact saved some witnesses' lives, were not embraced as essential parts of the story. Moreover, in media texts, the article in *Cho Sun In Min Bo,* written by the North Korean soldiers who had witnessed the incident, was not introduced with the same attention as other written documents generated by American troops. Thus, this first and most direct written account of the incident by North Koreans was not considered a significant source in U.S. media coverage.

Two elements seem to have obscured the episode of the North Korean soldiers in the No Gun Ri account. First, whereas some survivors explicitly addressed the aid of North Korean soldiers in remembering the incident, other survivors self-censored their testimonies to avoid getting their claims caught in ideological debates. For instance, Chung Koo-Hun related that he had not narrated his encounter with North Korean soldiers after escaping the tunnel until the researcher interviewed him in 2005. With the same cautiousness, Yang Hae-Suk asked me not to cite her comments on the North Korean soldiers if no other narrators mentioned it. Although the end of the Cold War era mitigated the political tension in South Korea, survivors who were victimized in the war did not seem to be free from their deeply ingrained fears of political ideology. This self-censoring of testimonies underscores oral historians' arguments that no memory agents—not even ordinary, local people—are free from discursive and ideological forces.[45]

A second reason for the omission of the episode of the North Korean soldiers is that the images of North Korean troops in the survivors' testimonies diverge from archetypical images of communism in American collective memory of the Cold War era. In the dominant narrative of the Korean War, in which American soldiers were on a mission to save Koreans from Communist invasion, North Korean soldiers appeared as Soviet-inspired, inhumane troops who took civilians hostage. This created a one-sided perception of the incident in which loathing of communism replaced a careful examination of the tragedy. One reader wrote: "Those civilians died because the country of North Korea had brutally and viciously launched a bloody assault on their country."[46] This absolute condemnation of communism emerged even in some of the Korean survivors' testimonies, revealing the similarity between official narratives in the American collective consciousness and in the South Korean collective memory of the war.

Although the U.S. media frequently used the term "Communists" in reference to clandestine groups who provoked fear, when forming the "fear-stricken soldiers' defensive action" narrative, the media barely introduced the local context of Korean communism, the essential key to understanding the background of the war. Many historians argue that the exploitative policy of Japanese colonial rule nourished the development of Korean communism.[47] Fused with the spirit of the independence movement, communism became a popular as well as legitimate political idea among the young educated Korean population. In his study of a Korean farming village on the island of Kanghwa in 1947, Cornelius Osgood, an American anthropologist, wrote: "'Communist' has become a strange word in our time and it may refer to a political philosopher, a Russian spy, a member of any other political party, a labor organizer, a traitor to one's country, or someone who happens to be regarded as an enemy. On Kanghwa it seemed to mean just 'any young man of a village.'"[48] The counter-narratives about Korean Communists found among survivors' testimonies, historians' analyses, and anthropologists' witnesses have posed disturbing but necessary questions that need to be examined, including questions about the "communism" of teenage North Korean soldiers.

The analysis of No Gun Ri texts reveals that survivors' oral memories, despite their initiation of media coverage, were largely diminished in the media's narrative formation. In both official and media accounts, the frailty and complexity of survivors' memories were repeatedly noted in order to undermine the veracity of eyewitness accounts. Moreover, the fact that human memories are inevitably caught between "remembered experience" and "remembered conversation"[49] was not appreciated; rather, it was used to maintain the ascendancy of written documents over oral memories. Such devaluation of oral testimonies parallels conventional historians' tendencies to dismiss oral memories, citing their subjectivity and inferiority to documentary knowledge. However, I argue that memory's fluidity does not diminish the validity of human memories in historical accounts; rather, it calls our attention to the fact that the credibility of human memories needs to be evaluated using different criteria.

Human memories resemble archival images before the digital era. As edge-worn archival images invoke authenticity, survivors' wrinkled bodies and aging voices enhance their authority to look back at the past. Over time, archival images lose their saturation. Similarly, distance from the past may reduce the volume and clarity of human memories. Survivors' testimonies in No Gun Ri prove that human memories are faltering, discrepant, even conflicting with one another in specific recollections. Perhaps the mere collection of discrete memory pieces can draw only an enigmatic account that barely approximates the truth. Yet it is important to note that the very fragile memories related by No Gun Ri witnesses have provided us with both narrative and pictorial cues with which we can visualize an incident that we did not witness. Witnesses' memories thus become woven together not in a way that creates a completed story, but in a way that rings true. Through this process, the veracity of human memories emerges. *This veracity of human memories resides not in accuracy but in corroboration and in resonance.*

In addition to memory's veracity, the No Gun Ri story has encouraged us to recognize the truth of Halbwachs' insight that human memories are limited by both time (human life span) and space (spatial proximity). Surely the fact that the survivors reside in either the same or nearby villages has contributed to the maintenance of enduring memories. Unlike space, time has more complex layers in the case of No Gun Ri. By the time that the media began to expose the stories, many primary narrators—the U.S. commanders and the parents of the Korean victims who witnessed and understood the incident—had passed away. The lack of witnesses who had voluminous memories made the story of No Gun Ri more fragile.

Despite these limited conditions, the Associated Press had access to counter-memories from remaining survivors. One might argue that media technology has alleviated the influence of life span on collective memories. In fact, the media's No Gun Ri coverage demonstrates its potential to preserve memories as well as to extend the duration of human memories. No Gun Ri also indicates, however, that counter-memories encoded in media can be most subversive when accompanied by feedback from witnesses who initially provided those very counter-memories and who later pointed out what aspects of their stories were selected (or deselected) in media texts. My research supports this perspective. Without living witnesses, I would not have been able to unearth essential parts of counter-memories that have been largely obscured in media texts. Although modern media have increased their capacity for capturing and preserving memories, the human life span is still the critical factor in determining the vivacity of collective memories because it is the existence of witnesses that makes counter-memory texts subversive. In sum, this research underscores a point that *the existence of witnesses can optimize the subversive qualities of counter-memories.*

Finally, No Gun Ri substantiates memory scholars' consensus that the selection of memory takes place on two planes: remembering and forgetting. Moreover, this event illustrates that war narratives related to national identity are completed by the consensus not only of what to remember but also of what to forget. In particular, the comparison between narratives of media texts and those of survivors' testimonies enabled me to elaborate upon the plane of forgetfulness. *Forgetfulness takes place not in the absence of memories themselves, but in the absence of certain frames, perspectives, and contexts of memories.* No Gun Ri, a disturbing episode in U.S. national memory, had been forgotten because there were no such frames that could encapsulate such an incident in American collective memory of the Korean War. The barren landscape of the U.S. collective memories of that war could not embrace No Gun Ri survivors' testimonies, which featured alternative perspectives of the war based on cross-cultural encounters and local expressions of communism. Determined to ignore such contexts, the U.S. media have largely silenced survivors' counter-narratives.

When listening to narrators' lively recollections during the summer of 2005, however, I realized that the story of No Gun Ri was still looking for an outlet, not one that required an artificial closure but rather one that allowed the story to flow without ending. Perhaps it is a memory scholars' mission to illuminate as well as locate hidden memory sites and suppressed voices. By unearthing counter-voices beneath the contrived narratives of official memories, memory scholars not only can deepen their deconstruction of memory texts, but also can encourage an audience in the present to be a critical appreciator of the past. Whereas historians' mission is to create "an unending dialogue between the present and the past,"[50] I would argue that memory scholars in the communication field have an obligation to create a linkage between two disconnected memory construction sites: onstage (media texts) and backstage (sources; testimonies). When the official memories seamlessly package the fragmented counter-voices to accommodate hegemonic narratives, critical academic practice has to rupture such a contrived closing by unearthing plausible narratives from the silenced, forgotten, yet enduring repositories of counter-memories.

CHAPTER 2

"Scripting" Memories

Female Survivors' Witnessing the No Gun Ri Killings

In the summer of 2005, with the hope of grasping the No Gun Ri text on a deeper level, I conducted oral history interviews in South Korea with survivors and victims' relatives whose testimonies were the primary ones that were used in the U.S. media coverage of the No Gun Ri incident. I first encountered them at the memorial ceremony that took place in the very tunnel of the tragic incident. The No Gun Ri bridge that I witnessed in July of 2005 was no longer a secret, hidden, or silenced place. The memorial ceremony, organized by survivors and victims' relatives, was publicly advertised with brochures that invited villagers, artists, local officials, and journalists. In contrast to the memory of the chaotic tunnel with defiled bodies, blood, and groaning, the same space as a site for the memorial looked very orderly. I saw the bridge filled with people in suits, lined chairs, and a neatly decorated altar embellished with flowers and incense. There, I could recognize familiar faces whose photos had appeared in the U.S. media coverage of the No Gun Ri killings.

During the Joint Memorial Ceremony, a performance for the dead of the No Gun Ri killings (July 28, 2005)

Since the beginning of the interview process, No Gun Ri narrators welcomed me as an attentive listener to their stories as well as a potential conveyor of their trauma to the American public. It was clear that they hoped that my research would contribute to challenging the public amnesia in the United States that surrounded the No Gun Ri incident. They welcomed me to their homes, where I could encourage them to recollect the incident within their most comfortable context. As each narrator had a different volume of memories—memories that she wanted to share—the length of the interviews varied from about one and a half hours to three hours. The interviews took place with an incredible flow: once the narrators started, the long threads of their stories poured out like streams of water. I was convinced that these survivors were actually very experienced narrators who seemed to have had considerable exercise in relating stories through their past participation in interviews conducted by media practitioners as well as by official investigators.

During the interview process, I employed several techniques that oral historians have developed in order to balance the power between researcher and narrator. In particular, I strove to share the authority of structuring the interview process—the format, flow, and questions—with the narrators themselves. Although I prepared a basic questionnaire that provided subjects with guidance as well as evoked their memories of the incident, I let the narrators choose where to begin their long stories and in what part of the stories they took time for elaboration. This approach unexpectedly enabled me to recognize an incredibly skillful group of narrators of trauma: the female survivors of the No Gun Ri killings. As eloquent speakers of their war experiences, the No Gun Ri females contest the notion that males—because they traditionally are more involved in warfare—are more entitled or better equipped than females in communicating about war. In fact, the No Gun Ri females' testimonies suggest how women, unlike their male partners who highlight the historical and political backdrops of their memories, tend to *contextualize* trauma in terms of their relationships with loved ones as well as their location in the multiple settings of daily life and how by doing so, they become competent communicators of the complexities and intricacies of trauma. In addition, these women did not end their stories at the last day of the No Gun Ri incident; rather, female survivors became more intense and expressive when they recalled the days *after* the war. What has powerfully emerged from the female narrators' reflections upon the aftermath of war is the endurance of trauma.

Perhaps my societal identity, that of a female researcher who grew up in South Korea, could be somewhat conducive to interaction between myself and the female survivors. They seemed to acknowledge me not as one of the removed interviewers who was collecting their stories, but as one of their own kind who could relate to their identity as mothers in a Confucian culture and who thus would be more likely to validate their long-ignored trauma. It was also interesting to note that female narrators tended more than their male counterparts to make encouraging remarks about my identity as an academician. It gave me a sense that they might have recognized me as a symbolic icon who has vicariously fulfilled their longing for education, a goal that female survivors hardly could have achieved amid such turbulent life circumstances.

subthesis

The ultimate goal of this chapter is to deconstruct the ways in which female survivors witness their trauma. In their analysis of life narratives, Sidonie Smith and Julia Watson note that trauma is not merely remembered; instead it is an abstract cluster that can be "scripted and exorcised."[1] As they put it, "In autobiographical acts, narrators become readers of their experiential histories, bringing discursive schema that are culturally available to them to bear on what has happened."[2] Smith and Watson's insights have provided frames within which to examine how the texture of trauma has unfolded in rhetorical practice. I argue that the female narrators in the No Gun Ri story became vocal and eloquent because they were able to read and speak their trauma through the filter of motherhood, the most plausible script of women's experiences under the legacy of Confucianism. By securing narrators' locations (as mothers and mourners), the script of Confucian motherhood enabled female survivors to vehemently carry out their legitimate sorrows and pains. Reflected in Confucian heritage, however, the script also invited judgmental tonalities in the memories of female narrators. Furthermore, the No Gun Ri female testimonies suggest how effective the oral form of communication can be for describing trauma. In recalling the incident, survivors not only scripted their stories, but also exuded "inarticulable—and thereby deep" memories that oftentimes were incompatible with their narratives.[3] Granting narrators a variety of nonverbal means of expression, the oral form of communication not only facilitated female narrators' ability to exorcise inarticulable memories that could not be subject to scripting but also allowed them to manifest through their wounds the incommunicability of the repressed trauma.

The list of female narrators whom I interviewed included Park Sun-Yong, who lost both her five-year-old son and her two-year-old daughter; Chung Myong-Ja, whose mother and sister died and whose brother was severely wounded; Yang Hae-Sook, who lost her left eye and whose mother was seriously injured; Chun Choon-Ja, who lost her mother, brother, and grandfather; Chun Ok-Boon, an aunt of Chun Choon-Ja; and Keum Cho-Ja, whose right hip was disfigured in the incident. At the time of the No Gun Ri incident, female survivors' ages ranged from eleven to twenty-five. Except for Park Sun-Yong, who was a young mother with two children, five of the narrators survived the incident as daughters who witnessed their mothers' desperate protection of their children. Therefore, the identities of these narrators as mothers were forged not in the space of witnessing, but in the subsequent rhetorical space in which they have constantly reflected upon their memories of their mothers in the past while experiencing their own motherhood in the present. In the following section, I will introduce three types of stories identified in the testimonies of these female survivors. Each story reveals how the female survivors recalled their memories as a way of reflecting upon their thoughts as to what it means to be a good mother. I here remind readers that the survivors' testimonies in this chapter are presented in a culturally edited form that unavoidably reflects not only a linguistic incompatibility in the process of translating the words from Korean to English, but also the researcher's own cognizance in the process of selecting original utterances.

THE THREE TYPES OF STORIES

The first type of story is that of the *dedicated mother*. Mothers in the No Gun Ri incident in the past made the most concrete and vivid testimonies about the incident because they happened to witness detailed images with their vigilant eyes while they desperately attempted to protect their children from bombs and bullets. After more than half a century, however, these dedicated mothers have passed away. Many still-surviving narrators of the No Gun Ri incident were at that time children who barely survived beneath their parents' bellies and their neighbors' dead bodies. Chun Choon-Ja, who was eleven years old, recalled haunting moments of how she witnessed her loved ones killed at the incident:

> My mom was breast-feeding my baby brother [on the railroad]. Since she skipped several meals, her breast milk was dried up. She asked me to get her water. She seemed to believe that if she drank water, she could breast-feed her baby again. I was going to leave my mom to find water, but I couldn't. All of sudden, an airplane appeared making a big explosive noise. Ashes came down from the sky ... it was strangely dark. ... I couldn't see my family. Soon after, I found my mom dead ... she had been bombed on her head. My baby brother was still alive suckling my mom's dead breast. (Chun Choon-Ja, in an interview with the author)

In this testimony, Choon-Ja's mother appears as an emblem of a dedicated mother who wants her worn body to be dedicated to the survival of her baby, who was starving and distraught within the barren space of war. In the No Gun Ri story, a baby clinging to his dead mother's breast is a visual icon that shows how life and death are entangled with the civilians' vulnerable bodies amid the guerrilla tactics of the war. It is a montage that contrasts life (a living baby) against death (a dead mother) as well as a symbolic binding of loved ones that protects life (the family) against a villain (the war) that is destroying that bond.

As determined protectors of children, mothers often seemed to commit heroic actions. In another example of a heroic mother, Yang Hae-Suk proudly recalled how brave her mother was at the moment of the air strafing that took her left eye: "I had seen airplanes flying in the sky those days, but that was the first time that I heard such a loud sound from airplanes. Planes flying toward us walking along the railroad tracks poured out something like fire. They were flames of fire." In the next moment, she found that her mother was dragging her two younger brothers under an acacia tree. She quickly followed them. While the strafing continued, Hae-Suk's mother desperately protected her sons and daughter from the barrage of bombs by covering them with her own body. Hae-Suk recalled that her pregnant mother lay facedown with her two sons underneath her stomach. From fear, Hae-Suk also was hiding herself inside her mother's hemp skirt. When the sound of bombs exploded near them, Hae-Suk began to hear her mother's groaning. Her mother had been severely wounded on her legs, but she did not change her position of covering her children.

For Hae-Suk, the world outside her mother's hemp skirt became gruesome. She was devastated at seeing her uncle's body torn apart right outside her mother's skirt. At the very moment that she heard her mother saying, "Why don't you lie on your face?" she felt something burning in her left eye. Hae-Suk said, "I cried out to my mom, saying 'Mom, fire hit my eye . . . something keeps coming out of my face.' I couldn't see anything. . . . I couldn't even see things oozing out from my eye." With the help of other refugees, Hae-Suk, her mother, and her two younger brothers barely made their way to the No Gun Ri bridge. Underneath the bridge, the baby brother died, but Hae-Suk and her younger brother, Hae-Chan, survived. Hae-Suk's mother had suffered with wounds until she passed away.

In both Choon-Ja's and Hae-Suk's memories, mothers appear as protagonists whose heroic actions not only guided their children on the chaotic battlefield, but also ultimately helped their grown-up children to make sense of fragmented images and words in their recollections of the war. Moreover, the plausibility and poignancy of motherhood as a cultural script empowered the female rhetors to be vocal about how the war had actually devastated their loved ones as well as themselves. Evoking a sacred icon of Pietas, the No Gun Ri stories thus have become a robust collection of antiwar statements that commemorates dedicated mothers who heroically fought against the violence, destruction, and death that the war had created.

The second type of story is that of the *disappearing mother*. A fierce war does not always render females good mothers in the eyes of their culture. There were females who could not fulfill their society's lofty expectations of motherhood. Keum Cho-Ja was one of the victims shot by American machine guns that had been aimed at refugees who were frantically running for cover behind trees and rocks when the air strafing began on the railroad. She was twelve years old at that time. When the bombs fell on the railroad, she, her mother, her younger brother, and her sister ran into a small cave near the No Gun Ri tunnel. However, as happened to many families, Cho-Ja's family was driven out of the cave and onto the street by the shooting: "As I followed my mom fleeing from the cave, I got a shot here"—she pointed to a ball-sized lump on her hip—"See, I have a bump here. . . . I saw my intestines come out from this spot."

Cho-Ja cried for her mother, but she could not stop her mother to get her to take care of her wounds. "I shouted, 'Mom, I got shot' . . . however, my mom, carrying my brother on her back and my sister on her side, did not slow down her walk and told me, 'If you can follow me, follow me.'" It was not possible for Cho-Ja to follow her mother, who walked as fast as possible to save her other two babies. Ironically, with the help of American soldiers, Cho-ja made it home safely. Later, Cho-Ja's mother, who had abandoned her during their flight, also returned home with her two babies. Although everyone survived, Cho-Ja's family was no longer the same as it had been before the incident. Cho-Ja's father harshly blamed his wife for leaving her wounded daughter behind alone. Cho-Ja said, "It was the first time that I saw my father slap my mom's cheek. He yelled at my mom that she should never have left her own child behind even if she herself would have died."

Like her father, Cho-Ja found herself distanced from her mother. Since the incident, a hurt feeling of abandonment has kept Cho-Ja from repairing the relationship with her mother. Also, her wounded body, a bumpy scar on her hip with no feeling, has hurt her relationship with her husband throughout their marriage: "Whenever he drank, I had to hear him saying, 'I got married to a deformed girl.' I could not respond to him for thirteen years until he died." That was the first and last marriage in her life. As a single mother, Keum Cho-Ja has raised four daughters by herself. She has worked as a door-to-door saleswoman peddling different articles, from tofu to fish. She never left her daughters alone until they all found their soul mates and settled down in happy marriages.

Like the stories of previous narrators, Cho-Ja's story revolves around the theme of motherhood. Motherhood in Cho-Ja's story functions as a strong rhetorical device that makes sense of both her traumatic memories and their influence on her life. Yet, in Cho-Ja's testimonies, what made Cho-Ja's mother leave her own child behind remains unclear. Cho-Ja, however, heard that when her mother was trapped in the barrage of shots with responsibility for three children, a neighbor next to her quickly gave her the advice: "Your daughter seems to be shot badly. She won't survive. Let's leave here quickly to save your son." Despite her efforts, the story of Cho-Ja's mother seems to echo the didactic message that women should not abandon their loved ones in any situation, even if they are on the verge of losing their own lives. Women who failed in this lofty mission will not be recalled with pride. Rather, such survival will be remembered as a stigmatizing mnemonic that reminds the next parental generation of what they should not do.

The third type of story is that of the *survived mother*. Here is another story about persistent motherhood. Park Sun-Yong was twenty-five years old. She is one of the few surviving parental witnesses. She lost her five-year-old son, Goo-Phil, and her two-year-old daughter, Goo-Hi, at No Gun Ri. She recalled the moment of the air strikes, an inferno-like scene on the railroad—"a dead cow spouted out a bloody flame," "bullets flew through the air like streaks of rain," and "people kept falling down dead"—as if she were still on those railroad tracks. Her words were stirring. When she arrived inside the tunnel, Sun-Yong found her sleeves had turned red with blood from her arm, which had been wounded by debris, but she did not feel any pain: "I was just so happy to see that my babies, such poor creatures starving all day under the hot sun, were still alive." This incredible joy that numbed her physical pain, however, did not last. At sunset, her mother-in-law, who was carrying her two-year-old daughter, Goo-Hi, told Sun-Yong that her little girl had just been shot in the neck at the entrance of the tunnel. "I became insane . . . I felt like my soul was departing me," said Sun-Yong. For the rest of her life, Sun-Yong never asked her mother-in-law the details of how her baby daughter was shot.

At dawn the next day, Sun-Yong decided to escape from the tunnel, as she could see no hope for her only remaining child, Goo-Phil. She woke up the servant boy, Hong-Ki, had him carry Goo-Phil on his back, and they all left the tunnel. When they were about to reach the bottom of the mountain, a crackle of shooting came toward them. Frightened, the servant boy left Goo-Phil and ran away alone. Sun-Yong found that bullets had torn a big chunk of flesh off of Goo-Phil's thighs. Grasping her wounded baby with one arm, Sun-Yong tried to walk again, but the bullets were pouring along the way. She recalled a flash of memory: "I saw a black soldier shooting toward us . . . then, a bullet hit my abdomen. It seemed that the same bullet went through my son's body." Waiting for death, Sun-Yong was lying still on the hill. Her baby Goo-Phil was lying beside her. Later on, they were approached by American soldiers, who buried Goo-Phil's dead body on the hill and took Sun-Yong to a modern military hospital. Since that day, she has never returned to the No Gun Ri area where her baby was buried. In her memories, it was she who should have saved her children from the lethal weapons. She said, "It was my fault. I killed them. If I were protecting them better, they wouldn't have died. It was my responsibility." Despite public recognition of No Gun Ri, her own guilt has never seemed to fade away.

FEMALES, THE PRIMARY WITNESSES OF THE NO GUN RI KILLINGS

During the interviews, what struck me the most was the vivid utterances of the female narrators about their own traumas. Traditionally, women's voices have not been included in war literature because "women are presumed to be absent from war."[4] Such a presumption about women's absence in war not only denies their actual presence as both civilians and soldiers on the battlefield, but also symbolically eliminates "the proof of being there," which Zelizer argues would give speakers the authority to relate their war stories.[5] Yet the vocal female narrators of the No Gun Ri story resisted the conventional idea that women are either silent or modest rhetors in an androcentric discourse of war. In the No Gun Ri case, women were surely the primary witnesses of the killings, since most patriarchs had already left their homes before the village turned into a battlefield. The extreme polarity of political ideology during the Korean War placed the status of patriarchs in a highly vulnerable position. Although they were not associated with any political position, the harsh battlefield reality forced even ordinary Korean males to take a stand on one side or the other. Thus, family members all together were vigilant in protecting patriarchs, including the lives of young males who would be the future patriarchs and therefore would carry on the family heritage as well as the lineage. In fact, when caught underneath the No Gun Ri bridge, elders and family members encouraged young males to escape from the tunnel. With their families' support on the first night under the bridge, several young males did succeed in making their way out of the tunnel. The elders, women, and children did not dare follow them because they worried that their clumsy movements would interrupt the young men's rapid escape.

After the flight of the young males, one of the female survivors, Chung Myong-Ja, recalled that the tunnel was full of women and children. She particularly remembered the presence of two female cousins who later died in the tunnel: "I was too young to follow the male escapers, but my female cousins could have escaped from the tunnel with the male adults; then they would be alive now. I am so sorry for their deaths at such a young, beautiful age" (in an interview with the author). Without patriarchs, the women had to go through the nightmare of these three nights and four days during which they desperately sought any protection for the children. It is interesting to note that in the context of war the somewhat paradoxical concept of manhood in Confucianism forced women to be the sole protectors of their children and—among those who survived—to be the primary witnesses to detailed images that the patriarchs never saw.

Nonetheless, seeing or experiencing does not always result in bearing witness. It is not easy for witnesses of traumatic events to reconstruct the story of an incident because, as many scholars argue, traumatic memories (i.e., images etched in their bodies and minds) are "unreadable," "unsayable," and "incommunicable."[6] Moreover, rhetors in trauma are caught in a paradox in that since the time of the disturbing events, they have been asked to relate the deadly moments of trauma (destructiveness) via their living, perhaps ever-recovering bodies (constructiveness). Thus, as Cathy Caruth puts it, we would benefit from analyzing the utterances of survivors within a sense that death and survival are equivocally and yet inexplicably intertwined in their traumatic experiences: "Trauma is not simply an effect of destruction but also, fundamentally, an enigma of survival. It is only by recognizing traumatic experience as a paradoxical relation between destructiveness and survival that we can also recognize the legacy of incomprehensibility at the heart of catastrophic experience."[7]

Having arisen from a paradoxical junction between death and survival, the fragments of traumatic memories are blended together in a chaotic manner. In fact, during the interviews, I sensed that the No Gun Ri females' memories consisted of fragmented images and sounds such as foreign language, menacing commands, torn and swollen flesh, and the bursting noises of shooting and bombing. What also struck me was that the survivors did not seem to lose their way amid such a maze of memories. They instead were skillful and composed rhetors who were capable of transforming entangled wads of "unspeakable" memories into lucid, "speakable" ones.

SCRIPTING "UNSAYABLE" MEMORIES WITH MOTHERHOOD

Images and sounds of trauma are often incomprehensible. They are primarily archived in living, yet wounded survivors' bodies and minds. Therefore, it is the survivors themselves who have exclusive and intimate access to reservoirs of unsayable memories. Yet such a privilege of access to reservoirs bestows upon survivors the unique burden of relating "suffering that defies language and understanding."[8] Perhaps post-traumatic stress disorder is not a condition of illness, but a reflection of "our inability to allocate meaning to the event."[9] It is also critical to note that survivors' witnessing trauma is paradoxical, because on the one hand the deed *decodes* memories (substantiating the utterance of trauma by scripting the memories with sets of narratives), and on the other hand the action *encodes* memories (weakening the utterance of trauma by arranging the memories with limited linguistic signs and structures). As narrators performing such a paradoxical act, survivors somehow seem to find a unique way to navigate the complex sea of memories. Survivors locate, identify, and discover cultural scenarios that make sense of their memories, particularly to other members of society who otherwise could not easily fathom the depth of their trauma.

No Gun Ri survivors in particular have spoken under the legacy of Confucianism. Since the Choson Dynasty (1392–1910), Korea has adopted Confucianism as a ruling state ideology. Having indoctrinated the virtues of filial piety as well as rigid hierarchical relationships based on gender, age, and class, Confucianism in Korea has functioned as a cultural and political apparatus that has fostered absolute obedience to the elder, the patriarch, and the state. In Confucian culture, a woman is confined to a patriarchal family that permits her only "a contingent identity as wife and mother."[10] The central role of women is to look after their husbands and parents-in-law with the virtue of submission and to nurture children with selfless dedication. Especially, given the Confucian patrilineage, the most expected duty for a woman is to give birth to sons who will carry on the family lineage as well as the heritage. Thus, a son resides in the core of a mother's identity. Only by producing and nurturing sons will her duties as wife and mother be fully credited.[11]

Such traditional values of Confucianism are still deeply entrenched in modern South Korea. In the process of rapid modernization South Korea has rejected some Confucian concepts, such as monarchical government and anti-commercialism, that are incompatible with the path to capitalism, yet the nation has still maintained the traditional norms of social and family relations.[12] As a salient example of surviving values, the Confucian notion of gender roles (i.e., the male as breadwinner and the female as reproducer) has been well preserved as an effective support for patriarchal ideology that naturalizes the gender-discriminatory labor market in the process of economic mobilization.[13] In particular, modern gender hierarchy in South Korea has been consolidated with the male-only military conscription, an institution that has reinforced the notion of gender division between "dependent housewife" and "provider husband."[14]

Such a strong legacy of Confucianism in modern South Korea has been the cultural context for the upbringing of the No Gun Ri female narrators. Throughout their lives, they have been taught the virtue of self-deprecation, one of the Confucian notions of womanly behavior that asserts that a chaste woman is not supposed to "make her concerns, let alone her feelings, known to others."[15] In keeping with these somewhat extreme, yet popular expressions of womanly behavior, traditional Korean society has reminded women that they deserve being divorced by their husbands if they commit any of the seven evil actions: "failure to give birth to a son; disobedience to parents-in-law; talkativeness; stealing; jealousy; adultery; and hereditary disease." Any of these transgressions can validate a husband's initiation of divorcing his wife.[16] Given this tradition, women are taught that reticence rather than talkativeness is a virtue.

Besides Confucian virtues, the male dominancy in contemporary war discourse also has contributed to the presumption that women are modest speakers in communicating any aspects of war. Thus, witnessing the killings at the No Gun Ri bridge has required the female narrators to break through dual conventions that are imposed by both Confucian codes and the androcentric discourse of war. Yet it is worth noting that the skepticism in Korean society about women's authority over speaking could motivate female narrators to seek out means that legitimize their voices.[17] Ironically, the No Gun Ri female survivors did work to locate means that were available to them within those very traditional values that restrained their voices. They have voiced their trauma through the script of Confucian motherhood. As mothers whose identities are solely secured by their dedication to reproducing and looking after their families, the No Gun Ri female survivors have adamantly spoken out against the war that challenged them to fulfill such critical duties. In other words, the script of Confucian motherhood (i.e., mothers as reproducers, protectors, and expendable assistants of the male blood line) has strongly positioned females as legitimate mourners who are entitled not only to vehemently cry out over the loss of loved ones but also to rightfully partake in the act of soothing their pain and sorrow.

Moreover, the women's witnessing of No Gun Ri inevitably resulted in actually altering the script of Confucian motherhood. While a chaste woman under Confucian codes is expected to practice and claim her motherhood in a private, secluded corner of the family circle, the No Gun Ri female narrators have let their images and words be widely displayed through the media, which has brought their untold stories to the attention of international audiences. In witnessing the killings, therefore, the female narrators have transformed a reclusive motherhood into a demonstrative motherhood that publicly pronounces their unyielding prerogative to protect their loved ones. As unreserved speakers, the female narrators have performed in public spaces an intense lament for their losses. Such adamant testimonies have also echoed dissident voices that denounce the government's long repression of counter-memories of past events. It is an ironic moment when Confucian motherhood, though altered, has contested another Confucian notion of filial piety: absolute obedience to the state.

MOTHERHOOD AS A DOUBLE-EDGED RHETORICAL DEVICE

The memories of the female survivors seemed to have achieved a degree of articulation when their stories were juxtaposed against the Confucian theme of motherhood that upholds good mothers as those who are reproducers and protectors of children (especially of sons). Characterizations of mothers in the females' testimonies are uniform in that they portray the incredible dedication and courageous actions that these women took to protect their sons: a mother who was looking for water only to enable her destitute body to breast-feed her starving baby son (Choon-Ja's story); a mother who shielded her sons underneath her stomach and would not budge even after fragments of bombing wounded her body (Hae-Suk's story); a mother who left her injured daughter behind to take her sons out of a dangerous battlefield as fast as she could (Cho-Ja's story); and a mother who fearlessly escaped the tunnel to spare her son from seemingly unavoidable carnage (Sun-Yong's story). Certainly, mothers are the protagonists of these female survivors' stories, whereas their desperate actions for saving their sons constitute the axes of these stories through which the rest of their memories are interwoven and clarified.

Furthermore, the mothers' selfless acts of rescuing sons from the harsh battlefield were often assisted by the daughters. Young females during the war were expected to take a supporting role in protecting their baby brothers. This expectation reflects a notion of filial daughters in the Confucian family. Under the patrilineage, daughters had no rights: "because they were expected eventually to marry out of their families, they were expendable."[18] An archetypal story of the filial daughter describes the time of modernization, when many young Korean females from rural areas worked in sweatshops in Seoul in order to financially support their families, and especially to help their brothers to get higher education. Such themes of the filial daughter are also found in Myong-Ja's testimonies of No Gun Ri. She was eleven years old when she witnessed her mother's death in the tunnel with her younger sister and brother. As one of the most indelible images, Myong-Ja described the scene of her younger sister, Young-Sook, climbing down their dead mother's back and searching for her breasts out of hunger, while her younger brother, Goo-Hak, with a bleeding face, kept crying out for water. On the last day, as the survivors made their way carefully out of the tunnel, no one was really willing to take care of these children who were left without parents. Myong-Ja returned home alone, leaving her baby sister in the tunnel along with her younger brother, who everyone said would not survive. It may not be surprising that Myong-Ja's return was not ardently welcomed. The eleven-year-old girl was blamed for not bringing her younger siblings home. She was a survivor, yet one who failed to fulfill the duty of a filial daughter. Since then, Myong-Ja continuously has felt a distance from her own family, who remind her constantly of her guilt. Worse, the aftermath of the incident has gradually weakened her body. "Sometimes I imagine," she related, "what if I had never survived in the tunnel during that time?"

Such testimonies suggest that Confucian motherhood—in its identification of women as reproducers, protectors, and expendable assistants of male blood lines—can be a double-edged rhetorical device in communicating trauma. On the one hand, the concept of Confucian motherhood has enabled the No Gun Ri female narrators to articulate their otherwise unspeakable memories; on the other hand, it has provoked the female narrators to judge their own and their loved ones' experiences in the war through the filter of a strict code of morality that leads to guilt and blame. As the most conspicuous example of such duality, Sun-Yong recalled the deaths of her babies with parallel narratives. First, she roared as a mother with indignation over the injustice that took the lives of her children: "American soldiers must have considered us no better than scum; otherwise they could not have undertaken such cruelty as killing those poor

babies." Perhaps the death of her own children is the most difficult mem- ✓✓✓
ory for a female witness to bear.

Second, and quite paradoxically, Sun-Yong related her stories with a composed voice, but one riddled with guilt. I doubt that she would ever have been able to communicate her trauma if she had not located both herself and her stories within the theme of Confucian motherhood. In this calm tone, she expressed a deep remorse by holding herself account-able for the deaths of her children. What struck me was that not until recently had she agreed to revisit the No Gun Ri bridge, which still retains the bullet holes with their stark evidence of what killed her babies. Nor did she attend any of the memorial ceremonies that have taken place under the No Gun Ri bridge since the AP's report. It seems that she was taking a pilgrimage not to the bridge with the bullet holes but rather to her own body and mind, which are scarred with self-blaming. In such rhetoric of guilt, the culpability is directed not to the inhumanities of war but to the mistakes of individuals (often family members and often the speaker herself) that resulted in the loss of loved ones. In brief, the script of Confucian motherhood appears to be a two-edged rhetorical device: it enables female narrators to speak up at times with an indignant, even dis-sident tone, yet it still infuses the women with a harsh self-judgment that disregards their efforts to be good mothers or filial daughters and keeps them from reading and speaking about war as a fundamentally inhuman, destructive apparatus.

EXORCISING "INARTICULABLE" MEMORIES WITH ORALITY

Although the very process of articulating trauma may trigger mixed sen-timents of anger, disapproval, and culpability among female narrators, scholars have noted that it can also offer mental healing and even cathar-sis to them. In her analysis of females' autobiographical writings, Suzette Henke elaborated on this process by coining the term "scriptotherapy," which refers to "the process of writing out and writing through traumatic experience in the mode of therapeutic reenactment."[19] Supporting Henke's point, Smith and Watson state that "speaking or writing about trauma becomes a process through which the narrator finds words to give voice to what was previously unspeakable."[20] Henke originally emphasized that a written form can be liberating particularly to female subjects because it allows them to publicly inscribe their personal stories onto the text, a traditionally patriarch-dominated medium.

Unlike Henke's subjects, however, No Gun Ri females have shared their stories not through writing but through speaking out. During the time of the Korean War, women in agricultural areas of South Korea were unaccustomed to expressing themselves through written forms of communication. It is not surprising that almost every written testimonial record regarding the No Gun Ri incident has been produced by either male survivors or male relatives of victims. For example, the first book about No Gun Ri was written by Chung Eun-Yong, whom villagers tremendously respected as a man with an outstanding education as well as high integrity. Yet the primary story of his book was based on his wife's (Park Sun-Yong) recollection of what she witnessed. Chung Eun-Yong was not in the village when the killings took place. Like many other young male patriarchs, he had decided to flee before his village turned into a battlefield. Right before the incident, he left his family behind: his wife, Sun-Yong; a son, Goo-Phil; and a daughter, Goo-Hi.

In various interviews (including one with the author), Chung Eun-Yong narrated in the first person, as if he had been at the scene, what his wife, Park Sun-Yong, and his children had to go through while he was not with them. The husband and wife were apart from each other during the incident, but they seemed to dwell together even as one memory agent in recalling the No Gun Ri killings. It is worthwhile to note that although he did not witness the incident in 1950, Eun-Yong was for more than five decades the only one attentive to how the traumatic memory had brought endless suffering to his reticent wife, Sun-Yong. After several years of witnessing his wife's sleeplessness every night, Eun-Yong said in an interview with the author that he had decided to let people know of her traumatic memories by writing a book titled *Do You Know Our Pain?*[21] Sensing the easing of the Cold War ideology in South Korea, he finally published the work in 1994. Certainly his book has played a critical role in transforming the No Gun Ri story from a local memory in a rural village in South Korea into a counter-narrative contesting the international memory of the Korean War. Without Eun-Yong's book, the story of No Gun Ri may have lingered amid his wife's sleepless nights and nightmares.

As reflected in the story above, the written narrative within the context of lingering Confucianism could be viewed as a patriarchal medium to which females would have access only through their male partners. Oral testimonies thus have been the exclusive means through which No Gun Ri female narrators have been able to convey their stories to many attentive listeners, including their family members, journalists, officials, and scholars from both the United States and South Korea. The No Gun Ri case confirms the recognition of many oral historians that the oral medium has been more powerful than any other medium in preserving as well as disseminating vernacular memories that are often found in the voices of voiceless and firsthand witnesses.[22]

Besides sheltering and cultivating vernacular memories, I also learned from the interviewing process that the oral form of communication provides narrators who have survived trauma with more inclusive means of expression—both verbal and nonverbal—through which they can let out inarticulable memories. As Young notes, eyewitnesses are "not testifying to 'what happened,'" but to what they saw.[23] Thus it is likely that eyewitnessing is a rhetorical practice that transforms abstract images caught in one's past sights into concrete terms available in a current society. Yet there are substantial images that cannot be easily conveyed through a coherent narrative, not even through a potent script like motherhood. For example, oral historians have noted that when female narrators try to express alternative concepts that do not fit dominant meanings, they often mute their own thoughts and feelings.[24] Muteness in oral testimonies is not considered to be a discontinuity of stories, but rather a reflection that a polysemous image (an original form of memory) cannot be expressed through words alone.

In the No Gun Ri case, however, female survivors hardly muted themselves. Regardless of the duration of the interview, they were lively, expressive, and fully present up to the final word. In particular, they continuously broke through the moment of incompatibility between images and words in testifying trauma. In fact, the constraint of words in oral communication seemed to force these narrators to more aggressively use a wide range of nonverbal means of expression, which resulted in their engaging with the past in a more dramatic, intimate way. During the interviews, I noticed that the female narrators, either unconsciously or consciously, exuded their feelings through multiple communicative modes, which included a variety of body movements, fragmented sounds, sporadic pauses, and facial expressions.

As the most dramatic nonverbal action, several survivors voluntarily exposed their wounds, the living mnemonics of trauma that continuously have been remolded through their aging bodies. They recalled how wounds stigmatized and humiliated them, in both public and private spheres, and how hurtful experiences taught them that the display of wounds would provoke only disdainful looks and treatment from others. For more than five decades, the No Gun Ri female narrators have practiced the masking of their wounds. In witnessing their trauma, however, they have willingly drawn interviewers' attention to the wounds as visual proof of their testimonies, as inexorable indictments of the war that unjustly consumed their bodies and psyches, and finally, as voices over the inexplicability of trauma through vocality alone.

Masked wounds seemed to become unmasked, especially when the female narrators felt pressured to condense their stories within limited, allotted times. Hae-Suk, who lost her left eye at the incident when she was thirteen years old, recalled how she could not resist exposing her private wounds to public eyes during her trip to America. She was among the six survivors and victims' relatives who came to America in the fall of 2000 to participate in a reconciliatory prayer service in Cleveland that was organized by the National Council of Churches; with the others, she also attended a news conference at the Pentagon. She recalls, in a discontented tone: "At the Pentagon, each of us was allowed to have only twenty minutes to speak. Do you think it's possible to tell our story within twenty minutes?" Her deep frustration sparked her to take a surprising action in front of the officials: "I am a very proud lady. I never showed my glass eye to anyone. But in the Pentagon, I couldn't fight my anger. . . . My voice was choked, I couldn't tell things, I couldn't hurry my words. So, I pulled out my eye, and put it on the table!" Her exasperation exploded again when the Pentagon investigative teams came to the survivors in South Korea. An advisory panelist documented Hae-Suk's ire in an account of his impressions of the No Gun Ri inquiry:

Seated across a long table opposite a dozen Koreans in a municipal building in Yongdong, a few miles from No Gun Ri, we heard tales of horror. Most of the Koreans with whom we talked had been children in 1950, but their memories, while inconsistent in some instances, had the ring of truth. . . . A stunning and unnerving moment came when one woman, now middle-aged, plucked a glass eye from its watering socket and exclaimed, "This is what I have lived with all these years." When we left the interview, so did our sense of detachment. We were a subdued group.[25]

Hae-Suk's action expounds an inseparable link between trauma and body. By granting narrators immediate access to their wounds, the oral form of communication has enriched a rhetorical space of trauma where survivors' intense body gestures potently implicate the meanings that their words evoke. As semiotician Roland Barthes noted, visual utterances often can be anchored by verbal utterance in any rhetorical space.[26] Yet female narrators' nonverbal expressions are often solid enough to complement, complicate, and even contradict what was said in oral testimonies. In the survivors' oral testimonies, the power relationships between images and words seem to be contested if not reversed. By dialectically linking bodily signals with words, the No Gun Ri female survivors communicated not only coherent narratives but also paradox, irony, incoherence, and disjuncture, all of which are essential textures of traumatic memories.

In brief, the No Gun Ri females' testimonies show that the act of communicating trauma takes place through both scripting and exorcising. Although the script of motherhood (rhetorical device) has allowed the No Gun Ri female survivors not only to negotiate with given cultural norms but also to transform their "enigmatic" trauma into "intelligible" stories to which anyone can relate, the form of oral communication (rhetorical space) has enhanced the performative dimension of testimonies by providing narrators with the means to exorcise trauma, which cannot be entirely subject to the act of scripting. As noted before, scripting is therapeutic because it provides the narrators with an opportunity to associate words with seemingly unidentifiable images of trauma. I argue here that exorcising can elevate such therapeutic effects by enabling survivors to extend their access to their trauma, even to inarticulable ones. Thus therapeutic effects are not only the result of "articulation" but also the reward for "letting it out."

The No Gun Ri female survivors whom I met during the summer of 2005 were no longer mere victims of the traumatic incident; rather they were vigorous narrators who actively navigated the incredibly complex sea of traumatic experiences. They also were skillful choreographers in a rhetorical performance in which they proficiently dealt with disparate paradoxes, tensions, and ironies that arose in the process of relating trauma: the narrators' enigmatic existence between death and the survival; their paradoxical acts of both encoding (substantiating) and decoding (emasculating) trauma; the tension between judgmental tonality and semantic plausibility in the script of motherhood; and finally the pull between images (bodily gestures) and words (narratives) in the oral form of communication.

Their remarkable eloquence is even more impressive when we realize the set of rhetorical constraints that prevented these women from being vocal narrators in the first place. Until the 1990s, the authoritarian regime of South Korea symbolically annihilated any stories that implied the killing of civilians by the U.S. or South Korean troops. The situation was not much different in America. Given the official account of the Korean War that glorified American troops as saving agents in 1950s Korean Peninsula, stories like No Gun Ri could hardly find any place in U.S. collective memories of the war. Although such political sensitivities have been alleviated to the point that No Gun Ri finally found media outlets, conventional codes from both the legacy of Confucianism and the androcentric discourse of war have not encouraged the No Gun Ri female survivors to initiate testimonies or to take as active a role as did their male partners in conveying their stories to others. As a clear example, Park Sun-Yong's memories, which make up the backbone of the No Gun Ri story, were not communicated by her; her memories at first were introduced only through her husband's writings. Even now, female survivors' public exposures (interview schedules) are mainly mediated by the No Gun Ri Committee, whose leadership comprises male survivors and male relatives of victims.

Remarkably, however, such rhetorical constraints have not muted the female survivors. Rather, as Campbell originally notes, prejudice against their stories and cultural expectations of modesty seemed to have motivated the female narrators to be more cautious about "how to voice" as opposed to "what to voice" in their testimonies. Particularly, the No Gun Ri female narrators have made use of the theme of motherhood to render their unbearable traumatic experiences as plausible and humanistic stories to which everyone, regardless of their political predisposition, could relate. With the Confucian script of motherhood, the No Gun Ri female survivors have successfully negotiated the given cultural norms, while turning themselves into vigorous narrators who read, script, and ultimately cry out their long-ignored sufferings to others.

The testimonies of the No Gun Ri females also corroborate that well-woven stories in memory construction render "the contingent and discontinuous facts of the past" to be "intelligible."[27] Through the process of transforming enigmatic texts of the past into plausible narratives in the present, female narrators have shifted their relationships with their own suffering. In the past, they were passive, even hopeless pain takers who could not resist the strike of suffering at the moment of the incident. Yet in their present recalling, they appear to deter the momentum of trauma by identifying and locating the implication of their suffering within the larger context of both their personal and their social lives. Most of all, through the implicated manifestation of their suffering, female narrators resist "the myth of a protected zone for women and children" that has been nourished in an androcentric discourse of the war.[28]

In contrast to the macro, hero-oriented statistical readings of war, the memories of female survivors, filtered through motherhood, have revealed how a war can boldly and intricately devastate each individual's life. The testimonies of the No Gun Ri females also have exposed how scripting of memories can be subject to society's conventions that have produced the very script. The three types of stories—dedicated mother, disappeared mother, survived mother—have reflected to varying degrees the conventional narrative of patriarchal ideology: a polarization of motherhood to the heroic saga or to the guilty loss of loved ones. Although this process has empowered female narrators to articulate their unspeakable memories, scripting through Confucian motherhood has not brought immunity to the patriarchal ideology in constructing narratives.

Besides scripting, the No Gun Ri female narrators also have made an effective use of the nonverbal means of expressions that were largely available in the oral form of communication. Through their bodily performance (gesture, movement, and facial expression) and their low definition of vocality (stuttering, mumbling, pause, and muteness), survivors have exorcised (let out) their inarticulable memories that could not easily have been subjected to scripting. Their testimonies have reminded us that human bodies are the oldest, yet still the richest, medium for a complex subject like trauma, even among the dazzling list of new media. Most of all, it was thrilling to note that the survivors' exorcising through oral testimonies transformed their fragile bodies into the most formidable means for sternly indicting the very war that shattered those bodies. It was at the moment of overdue exasperation that the female survivors proclaimed their long-hidden trauma, and it was also at the moment of overdue reclamation that they restored the ownership (that is, the rights to read, speak, and mourn) of their own suffering that had been appropriated both by the war and by the androcentric discourse of the war.

Through this research, I have come to realize that what survivors really wanted to communicate with the rest of us was not necessarily what really happened in the past *but the perplexity of relating trauma in the present.* In fact, one can begin to communicate trauma only when he or she recognizes the inexplicability of traumatic experiences. As Caruth notes, the truth of trauma is linked not solely to "what is known" but also to "what remains unknown in our very actions and language."[29] Perhaps the enigmatic cluster of feelings that survivors exude through exorcising simple signals suggests that there are only tenuous rhetorical resources in communicating trauma. Perhaps the plausibility of female survivors' testimonies implies not how much they can articulate their trauma but how much we can grasp the trauma of others. To understand such a grasp more fully, one must peruse not only what was uttered but also how, in what context, against what constraint, and finally with what script and medium such traumatic memories have been communicated to us.

CHAPTER 3

"Sanitizing" Memories

Archival Images in the PBS Documentary
"Battle for Korea"

Unlike other wars, the Korean War resides not in the collective memory but in the collective amnesia of the American public consciousness. This "collective amnesia" of the Korean War is reflected in the unpopularity of cultural products and the paucity of academic discourse, as well as the absence of iconic images of this period in history, all of which render the Korean War a dormant memory text. The official account of the Korean War has surfaced too infrequently to be contested. Thus ironically, while the official accounts of other wars are strengthened through the repetitive manifestation of their narratives in the cultural discourse, the official account of the Korean War—in which the war has been framed as America's mission of saving Koreans from Communist aggression—has safely been maintained because there has been little chance of the account's being contested.

More specifically, there exist few cultural products in the United States that commemorate the Korean War. Perhaps the most popularly recognized vehicle is the TV show *M*A*S*H*. Although this program is set during the Korean

War, it is often confounded with memories of the Vietnam War. In fact, Loretta Swit, who performed as an army nurse in *M*A*S*H,* has served as a spokesperson for the Vietnam Women's Memorial Project.[1] The Korean War, caught between the Second World War and the Vietnam War, as historian Paul Pierpaoli puts it, "generated too little myth of its own."[2] As another example, in 1995 the Korean War Veterans Memorial was placed on the National Mall in Washington, D.C. Although recognition of the memorial has increased, I nonetheless argue that it is still a quiescent mnemonic object that has experienced a meek resonance. While the names etched in the Vietnam Veterans Memorial have provoked intense reactions from both public and scholars,[3] the slogan "Freedom is not free" engraved on the Korean War Veterans Memorial merely reinforces, with little resistance, the official narrative of the war by echoing the sacred sacrifice of American soldiers in Korea. Thus, the Korean War Veterans Memorial has not ignited any vivid discussion among academicians or the public.

It is important to realize that the Korean War has been unpopular both with the mass media and with scholars. While photographic images of the Holocaust were released from the Nazis' records, a large portion of Korean War images have been kept exclusively in communist countries until recently. Similarly, the Vietnam War has been discussed frequently among critical scholars, but the Korean War has been hidden behind the aura of the Cold War. Lingering McCarthyism in both the cultural and the political space, hidden archives in unconnected information channels, and closed dialogue between the North and South have made the Korean War an overtly sensitive issue, which in turn makes it difficult to develop commercial products about this event. In fact, the *Korean War Filmography,*[4] published immediately after the fiftieth anniversary of the Korean War, indicates that most of the films regarding the war came out in the 1950s and 1960s; since then, the war has been largely forgotten within the realm of popular culture.

The scarcity of cultural products during the postwar era has led to a lack of academic discourse concerning how the media have portrayed the Korean War. Most academic achievements pertaining to representations of war have discussed other wars: the Great War,[5] the Holocaust,[6] the Second World War,[7] the Vietnam War,[8] and the Gulf War.[9] But the lack of cultural products and discourse seems to have submerged the memories of the Korean War beneath the public consciousness. Howard Schuman and

Jacqueline Scott's report in 1989 indicates that it may be hard to resurrect the Korean War in American collective memory. They asked a national sample of adult Americans to report "the national or world events or changes over the past 50 years."[10] Results showed that while 21.3 percent reported the Second World War and 11.6 percent listed the Vietnam War, only 1 percent mentioned the Korean War.

This situation, however, is changing. The end of the Cold War era has opened a new chapter for the Korean War archives. In the early 1990s, when the Soviet bloc collapsed, Soviet archives that had been detained in the Kremlin began to be declassified. Furthermore, encouraged by "glasnost" policy, several former North Korean and Russian officers involved with the Korean War have published their memoirs about the war.[11] Moreover, newly released information about the Soviet and Chinese roles in the war introduced a long-ignored framework into the study of the Korean War: the communist perspective.[12]

In the West, archival sources have been more fluid. While a fire in 1973 at the National Personnel Records Center in St. Louis destroyed a substantial number of the individual files of soldiers who fought in the Korean War,[13] the Freedom of Information Act (FOIA) of 1975 has continuously allowed researchers to request access to government documents that do not belong to any exempt categories.[14] Now, five decades after the war, the sense of life passing has provoked many survivors, both soldiers and civilians, to step forward to share their hitherto untold memories. The most significant aspect of this new context is the influx of substantial counter-memories about the Korean War into various media. In the Korean War context, the historical facets that counter-memories would illuminate include the domestic class conflicts as a critical cause of the war, the U.S. atrocities toward Korean civilians before and during the war, the legitimacy of Korean local communism in the context of Japanese exploitive colonialism, and cross-cultural tensions, all of which are frequently found in the work of many historians but have barely resonated within the U.S. popular perceptions of the Korean War.[15]

Bruce Cumings, a renowned historian of the Korean War, points out that most literature of that war has been constructed mainly within official accounts and has not been contested by counter-narratives. Thus, he has tried to "recuperate the Korean war almost exclusively from primary materials."[16] Cumings particularly criticizes existing U.S. TV documentaries on the Korean War that have never been free from "unspoken rules of ideological discourse."[17] Although the context of memory has evolved now that ideological tension has drastically been reduced since the collapse of the Berlin Wall, there still exists an intense argument from progressive historians that the Korean War remains "a prisoner of the rigid mentality and ideology of the early Cold War."[18]

In this milieu, it is critical to look at media's rhetorical reconstruction of the Korean War because newly found archives have often arrived not in the territory of historians, but in that of mass media institutions. There is evidence that both visual and verbal archives are materials that are purchased, consumed, and circulated only by specific institutions that can afford these archival commodities. In other words, since greater economic power determines accessibility to archives, and the media have the greater economic power, then it follows that media practitioners will be likely to examine archives earlier than historians do. In fact, several documentaries came out right before and after the fiftieth anniversary of the Korean War. This list includes *The Korean War: Our Time in Hell* (Discovery Channel, 1997), *Battle for Korea* (PBS, 2001), *Korean War in Color* (Goldhil Home Media International, 2002), and *The Forgotten War* (ABC, 2003). The recent increase in cultural products about the Korean War in the United States reaffirms that media play a critical role not only in reconstructing the discourse of past events through piecing together newly found historical documents, but also in triggering our memory by leading us to interact with the repository of frozen moments from the past. Due to the burgeoning of media texts regarding the Korean War, more vigilance is required to examine what implications media institutions have uncovered from newly found archives, and how these institutions have translated those archives into narratives within the American collective memory of this war.

In order to explore such processes, this chapter undertakes a textual analysis of *Battle for Korea*, a film that was introduced through the Public Broadcasting Service (PBS), an avenue with a relatively substantial cultural authority to relate the stories of past events. Unlike commercial media institutions, PBS emphasizes educational and social purposes, and that focus has consolidated its cultural legitimacy as the producer of somewhat authentic representations of historical as well as cultural events. Such an emphasis could give viewers the idea that PBS may not be easily swayed by the desire to create compelling images from historical documents. Such a presumed credibility of the rhetor, however, often conceals the constructed nature of its cultural artifacts. Thus, I contend that PBS programs deserve a more careful look than do texts from commercial institutions. In fact, the more legitimacy the rhetor appears to have, the more critical scrutiny is required, because the illusory cultural authority can simply be used to naturalize the constructedness of narratives.

In addition to the reputation of PBS as an institution, archival images, which are film's primary materials, are another critical source that enhances a rhetor's credibility in *Battle for Korea*. The film, using newly arrived visual archives from the Soviet Union and China, is a 120-minute compilation documentary of black-and-white visual archives that relates the story of the Korean War from 1950 through 1953. It especially focuses on the military strategies and tactics that U.S. armies implemented during the war. Yet the military lens of the documentary seems too myopic to embrace the complex layers of the war. Given the context, the highlighting of military tactics even more strongly invites a rigid frame (the Cold War ideology), which perpetuates the dominant narrative of the Korean War: of the Americans' mission to save South Koreans from merciless communist aggression. Such a myopic ideological construction, I argue, has largely depoliticized newly found archives by blocking them from being connected to counter-narratives of the Korean War. In order to understand the intricate mechanism of how an ideological frame could constrain voices that have emerged from archival images, one should be aware of the syntax of images and their complex linkage with words in our act of remembering. Before deconstructing the text, I will discuss this relationship.

REMEMBERING THROUGH ARCHIVAL IMAGES

Since the invention of photography, the act of remembering has increasingly relied on visual documents: photographs, archival films, and video footage. Unlike verbal representation, image has a mimetic capacity that preserves as well as captures the moment of the event with great detail. Technology has continuously increased photography's denotative quality. This worried Roland Barthes,[19] a semiotic analyst, who was concerned that an enhanced mimetic quality would more effectively conceal the symbolic intentions of images.

Certainly, their denotative referentiality has allowed images to be the most powerful vehicles in the act of remembering. Memory scholars[20] agree that the mimetic capacity of images enables them to take over the primary role of stabilizing collective consciousness in terms of past events, as well as convincing a doubtful public about what occurred in history. Perhaps most important of all, the visual form of representation has a greater possibility of embracing counter-memory, because it exposes the facets of a complex reality that can hardly be wrapped in simplified and plausible narratives.

Interestingly, the syntax of image resembles memory. Scholars in visual communication have noted that while verbal language has a causal syntax in which words are arranged in order to form sentences or phrases, visual language does not have an explicit and determined syntax.[21] Information in images therefore is understood not by linear and logical sense-making but rather by non-linear and simultaneous assimilations. This process is very similar to that of constructing memory, in which the imagery of the past is understood by acquaintance. While freezing, resembling, and evoking the moment of past events, images themselves become a substantial memory rather than a mere vehicle of memory. Many scholars, however, have noted that although image allows us to experience a richer texture of the past, it can be vulnerable to commodity, propaganda, partiality, and decontextualization, particularly in contemporary visual culture.[22] This vulnerability of images has been exposed particularly in terms of its complex linkage with words. As Zelizer points out, it is not a mere word but a discursive framework of words that considerably determines the meaning of images.[23]

Scholars' analyses of the role of images in a cultural text have reminded us that image is not a plain mirror that reflects a puzzle of past events. Rather, it refracts as well as frames the moment of the past while interacting with available technologies, other symbolic apparatus, and given discursive frameworks. Thus the potential of image as a subversive vehicle for memory needs to be considered not only in terms of its representational potency but also within the perspective of its contextual fragility in the process of narrative construction.

The constructed nature of an image as a representational tool also has been elaborated in documentary works among scholars who have rejected the notion that photographic images can be objective or neutral.[24] According to these researchers, objectivity is simply an illusory goal in a biased process of non-fictional representation. Certainly, viewers' expectations of documentaries are different from their expectations of other genres. As Nichols notes, while fictional films trigger our desire for fulfillment, documentaries resort to our desire to know, a process that draws our attention to the epistemological dimension of documentary.[25] When a documentary covers a controversial issue, its viewing involves a discourse among producer, subjects, and viewers. With these recognitions, it is plausible to say that documentary is a visually mediated representation of reality in which biases from producers, subjects, and viewers are intertwined.

Nevertheless, this epistemological aspect of historical documentaries is often either neglected or simplified, consequences that have caused viewers to regard historical documentaries as simply objective depictions of past events. Questioning the cultural authority that the historical documentary has in telling history, this chapter will attempt to dissect the complex relations between images and words in memory construction. More specifically, the textual analysis of *Battle for Korea* will be conducted in two parts. First, we will look at how archival films function in the production of the film. *Battle for Korea* employs visual archives from China, Korea, the United States, and the Soviet Union. Some archives, according to PBS advertisements for the program, had never before been shown to the public. These rich visual documents make up sixteen sub-stories, all of which are chronologically deployed and provide the rationale for following this sequence. In addition to the visual archives, computer graphic images are used as secondary visual units. Their role is mostly to link adjacent sequences or to provide geographical and demographic information on military tactics. With the aid of such computer graphic images, we also shall explore how visual archives function on both the connotative and the denotative levels.

Second, this study will unpack the linguistic messages carried by the male narrator's voice, which dominates the film. Except for intermittent music, no supplementary sound is utilized. There are neither survivors' testimonies nor experts' interpretations. Even ambient sounds of images, which often result in a meaningful aural record that completes the meaning of visual images, have been minimized to an almost silent level. Certainly, the quality of audio recording technology at the time when the film included in the documentary was produced was less advanced than that of current video recording technology. Nonetheless, ambient audio noise, like an antique visual texture, can be an element that enhances historicity. Yet, throughout the program, *Battle for Korea* minimized all ambient sounds, thus increasing the monopoly of the dogmatic voice of the narrator. This salient linguistic message, as Barthes argues, efficiently sterilizes the polysemous quality of visual images by anchoring all possible meanings within a specific interpretation.[26] Thus, analyzing the voice of narration in terms of both its structure and its content will thoroughly reveal how the discursive frame adopted in *Battle for Korea*—the Cold War ideology—has constrained potential counter-narratives that have emerged from archival images, as well as perpetuated the official account of the Korean War (again, that Americans saved South Korean from merciless Communist aggression). The following section will elaborate this point with specific examples.

VISUAL STRUCTURE OF *BATTLE FOR KOREA*

With time, all photographic images obtain value as visual archives and become significant sources of collective memory and history. It appears that what was recorded visually receives greater attention than what was recorded in only a verbal form. Sometimes, both the academy and the mass media put their efforts into constructing visual memories from written records. Specifically, they undertake visual restorations of past customs, heritage, or events, most of which have appeared in written history books, but without corresponding visual images.

Despite an increasing passion for images, however, we do not equally value all images in our act of remembering. Rather, there exists a hierarchy of value among visual documents. Certainly, archival photos and films take a superior position in relation to two value-laden words: "authenticity" and "historicity." Yet many scholars[27] have warned that archival images should not be taken at face value, and thus the authenticity of visual materials needs to be questioned. Scherer argues that researchers should always evaluate photographs with regard to the following questions: "who took the picture, when, where, why (purpose for which it was taken), how (type of equipment used), who is in the picture and their reaction to being photographed."[28]

I doubt that the *Battle for Korea* employed visual archives with this careful scrutiny. Archival footage in this film came from various warring countries. It is possible that war correspondents from opposite sides photographed different images with differing compositions, reflecting their own country's point of view. For instance, many aerial views in *Battle for Korea* seem to be taken by the cameras of U.S. armed forces: an American ground post suffering from a hail of bullets; a U.S. airplane bombing the earth; and a U.S. aircraft carrier launching armed planes. These images certainly address who are the allied forces and who are the enemy troops of the United States, and show with which side the audience should place their sympathy. However, a considerable quantity of archive film in the program was obviously taken by correspondents on the Soviet side: close shots of leaders of North Korea, China, and the Soviet Union; captured American soldiers in North Korean military camps; North Korean soldiers training in their camps; enormous Chinese armies marching through the North Korean landscape; and so forth. Subjects in these visual archives never appear to resist being filmed. The camera shots are not sneaky, but direct and stable, implying that the photographers belonged on the same side as their subjects. Yet, regardless of their differing effectiveness, archives from opposing sides are never introduced as conflicting material. Rather, they are all used to convey the same perspective. In other words, the varying views encoded through different angles and frames have been melted into the totality of an image collection that was put together to privilege a dominant view of the Korean War. As a result, many visual archives in *Battle for Korea* are disconnected from the historical context in which they were born, and in the process they become fragmented icons. Ironically, history documentary, whose very purpose is to discover history, seems to undercut here the power of the historical utterances of these visual archives.

The manipulation of visual archives largely takes place in the editing process, which requires editors to make decisions about what to select and what to discard. In *Battle for Korea*, the selection of images results in three layers of visibility: highly visible, selectively visible, and invisible. First, the images of heroic figures are highly visible. *Battle for Korea* highlights many political figures related to the Korean War, including Mao Zedong, Joseph V. Stalin, Kim Il Sung, and Douglas MacArthur. Most important of all, the documentary spends considerable footage in introducing General MacArthur, who was a supreme commander of the UN forces in Korea. He is depicted here as the hero who had several important triumphs in the Korean War. The hero is an indispensable component when mainstream media depict the war. Like other war heroes, MacArthur in *Battle for Korea* is glorified with substantial narrative support as well as with tension-filled battle scenes. The narration tells us that MacArthur's perception of the Korean War was that the war was "an epic test of will between Communism and the West." In order to defeat the enemy utterly, MacArthur mounted several ambitious military campaigns, such as an amphibious assault landing at Incheon, along with the introduction of UN forces into North Korea. *Battle for Korea* thoroughly describes this mission of MacArthur with a spectacular visual combination of archival films and computer graphics. The climax of battle scenes provides viewers with tension and excitement. Gloomy film sequences of war are transformed into provocative and dramatic material. Many researchers of the representation of war criticize these compelling compositions of battle images for offering little insight into what the war means and for obscuring issues.[29] Moreover, the MacArthur "heroic" images in this film are not balanced by any visual counter-evidence or critically narrative voice. Thus, MacArthur, as portrayed in *Battle for Korea*, seems to be free from any criticism concerning his overly ambitious military actions, which increased soldier and civilian casualties.[30] In the end, *Battle for Korea* monolithically idealizes General MacArthur by introducing images of America's acclamation, even at the moment of his dismissal by the U.S. government: "On April 12, 1951, President Truman, with the agreement of the defense secretary, George D. Marshall, dismissed MacArthur from his job as supreme commander of the far east. The move would prove deeply unpopular with the American people. MacArthur was one of the United States' great military heroes. He returned to a hero's welcome and a storm of controversy" (narration in *Battle for Korea*).

Second, certain images are selectively used, such as those of civilians and soldiers. Eckert and his associates argue that Korean military and civilian casualties during the war are estimated at 2.8 million people.[31] *Battle for Korea* adds further information: that Chinese and American casualties numbered 1 million and 37,000, respectively. The tragedy of these millions of people could create a strong image of the atrocities of this war. The protagonists were deserted corps, fleeing refugees, marching armies, panicked faces—real people. Yet, in *Battle for Korea*, these actors are anonymous. They are visible mostly in collective shots in which individual beings are hardly identifiable.

The subjects are bundled together and objectified as either practitioners or targets of military tactics. Soldiers frequently are replaced with statistics, or represented by abstracted computer graphics. Civilians often are invisible when their lives were devastated by the numerous bombs that air forces vehemently dropped on them. The following narrations in *Battle for Korea* reveal such moments: "American and British aircraft carriers launched powerful strikes against the North Korean defenses. Rockets, bombs, and napalm rained down on coastal batteries and military installations." "B-29 Super Fortresses firebombed towns and villages in the northern part of North Korea." "The attack went on unabated throughout 1952 and burnt to the ground almost every city and town in North Korea."

The primary visual images along with the narrations above, however, are not the devastating consequences of bombings on human lives. Rather, viewers are invited to experience bombings from the pilots' point of view, where one can only marvel at the snazzy, video-game-like scenes of the air strikes. Such graphic imagery, though black and white, evokes a "highly stylized view of the war," reminiscent of the media coverage of the Gulf War.[32] Interestingly, archival images from the old war (Korean War) are reconstructed through a current template of war representation that was cultivated in the new war (Gulf War). The scenes of intense bombings on North Korean territory can be linked with counter-memories that the UN, the world's most universal peacekeeping organization, had devastated almost everything that the Korean people had inherited from their ancestors,[33] and that the U.S. military strategies during the Korean War were problematic in terms of handling civilians' lives near the battle zones.[34] Yet the visual construction of air strikes, with little iconicity of civilian casualties, does not really evoke those counter-narratives of the war. In brief, such an iconic annihilation of civilian casualties in North Korea provides strong evidence that the underlying discourse of *Battle for Korea* is the Cold War ideology, which contributed to the film's callous view of civilians in enemy territory (North Korea).

Battle for Korea is also missing some images. Photographers, correspondents, and journalists who had framed war images in the battlefield are never shown in the program. Although many print publications recognize the critical role of Western correspondents in representations of the Korean War,[35] *Battle for Korea* never shines light on their presence. Hudson and Stanier[36] argue that during the Korean War, Western correspondents paid too much attention to MacArthur's activity, and in the process failed to create iconic images from a civilian perspective. Such critiques explain why the Korean War is not represented by such iconic images as that of the napalm girl in Vietnam, an image that evokes a strong visual memory of civilian casualties.

Moreover, *Battle for Korea* never exposes the significant backstage context in which decisions about capturing who, what, and how were made. Only the shaky shots, taken near gun fighting, remind viewers of the photographer's presence behind the camera. The film's concealment of the backstage, as the criticism of many visual scholars reminds us, may blind viewers to the realization that what they see on the screen is not an accurate historical account, but rather a manipulated visual construction.[37] Allen suggests that when using visual archives in history documentary, filmmakers should inform viewers about who captured the images as well as how and where they found them.[38] It may be true that many visual archives are anonymous products. In this case, the origin of images can be communicated to viewers as "unknown."

One might argue that such an act of exposing the backstage by making visible those who capture the images will maintain the subversive power of documentary, a medium that provokes viewers to think "what it might be" as opposed to "what it is."[39] By examining the constructed nature of visual archives both in their creation and in their exposure, one may discern that it is impossible for the historical documentary to reconstruct a holistic and subversive synthesis of visual memories. Rather, we may encounter an arbitrary puzzle of available visual documents under the name of historical documentary. Only with conscious efforts to crack the codes will this epistemological pitfall become visible.

NARRATIVE STRUCTURE OF *BATTLE FOR KOREA*

As Nichols argues, even though we may think that history or reality is speaking to us through a film, what we actually hear is the voice of the text.[40] We hear this textual voice of documentary from both the physical voice of the narrator and the structure of narration. *Battle for Korea* has a typical narrative form as well as the structure of a conventional documentary. First, the film is guided by one voice-over, suggesting the narrative is as "true" as the univocal voice of "God." Considering that history is intrinsically in a state of debate, a single and unified narrative does not seem to be capable of telling history. This incongruity between polysemous history and univocal narrative form in history documentary, however, becomes invisible through an expressionless tone of voice that aims for objectivity. Toplin states: "Documentaries frequently deliver history through the voice of a formal interpreter whose confident narration suggests that all the facts are knowable and their meaning understandable."[41] *Battle for Korea* applies this rule by simply selecting the authoritative voice of a middle-aged male. The use of a resolute, even somewhat dogmatic voice implies that it would be hard for viewers to find any counter-narratives within the program.

Battle for Korea also has the typical narrative structure of a mainstream documentary. First, it reveals structural ambiguity. Whether it comes from the filmmakers' eagerness to reach a larger audience or is reflective of institutional efforts to achieve "objectivity,"[42] mainstream documentaries often apply ambiguous narratives in conveying controversial issues. The most popular way of building ambiguity within the historical documentary is to make humanistic and universal statements that can appeal to everyone, regardless of their point of view. Such statements usually are made in the closing narrative sequence. *Battle for Korea* is no exception. The following words are part of its conclusion: "In three years, one month, and two days of slaughter and destruction, almost two million Korean soldiers and civilians had died. A million Chinese had been killed or wounded. 37,000 Americans were dead. And after all the suffering, the warring sides were left almost exactly where they had begun. In the decades to come, North and South Korea would live on as two armed camps, facing each other over the most militarized and dangerous border in the world" (*Battle for Korea* narration). Closing the program with a humanistic, even somewhat nihilistic view is a cliché, but safe enough not to invoke harsh criticism from the audience. In *Battle for Korea*, the rhetorical ambiguity functions particularly as a political facade in its concealment of an essential character of the film: a rigid ideological construction of the war. As a result, the film gains the potential to reach a broader audience that would not necessarily recognize its conservative bias.

It is interesting nonetheless that it is the closing statement that finally creates a link between past and present, but such a link does not occur throughout the entire narration. The Korean War left not only records of destruction and casualties, but also indelible scars, fears, and insecurities that have been the most influential factors in Korean politics and culture. The memories of the war have also influenced the current U.S. relationship with North Korea, a regime that has continuously encouraged its own citizens to remember the U.S. atrocities toward civilians during the Korean War. Yet the voices of *Battle for Korea* have hardly triggered viewers' historical imagination over the dialectical link between past and present. As a result, visual archival images appear to be legendary, but no longer active memories. Such a rhetorical disconnection between the past and the present characterizes the site of memory not as a struggle of plausible narratives but as a solidification of the dogmatic narrative.

Causal explanation is another typical style of narrative structure in *Battle for Korea*. Every episode is structured by chronological causality, which artificially merges all contradictions and complexities into a linear progression from one point to another. This technique provides viewers with a simplistic and reductive way of looking at the past. One example is the narration used to explain the political turmoil in South Korea just before the war. After the withdrawal of Japanese colonial power, Korean society in 1945 was a maelstrom of various political forces with different ideologies. Colonialism had prompted class divergence and had spawned numerous resistance groups against the status quo.[43] This was one of the most critical moments in contemporary Korean history, and has been the focus of ceaseless debate among historians. Contrary to what one might expect of such a complex time, the narration in *Battle for Korea* describes this moment with very simple words: "Most Koreans were impatient for a united independent Korea and soon there were over 200 political factions in Korea all competing for power." In this narrative, the turmoil created by historically material conditions, such as class division and colonial experiences, is replaced with the abstract word "impatient." It is important to realize that this reductive narration has the potential to keep viewers from appreciating the dynamic contexts and subtleties that may be the key to understanding the complicated layers of history.

In addition to narrative convention, voices of historical texts also can be characterized by the force of institution. As Sturken puts it, "History can be thought of as a narrative that has in some way been sanctioned or valorized by institutional frame-works or publishing enterprise."[44] *Battle for Korea* was produced by Malin Film and Television, Ltd., in association with PBS (Public Broadcasting Service), broadcast through PBS channels and distributed by the PBS home video department. Defining the characteristics of PBS is necessary to analyze how institutional power is internalized in the audiovisual text of *Battle for Korea*. PBS is an American public network that is available to 99 percent of American homes with television (PBS Web site). PBS defines its identity with these words: "A trusted community resource, PBS uses the power of noncommercial television, the Internet, and other media to enrich the lives of all Americans through quality programs and education services that inform, inspire and delight."[45]

Thus PBS's goal is to target a broad range of audiences as well as to improve viewers' lives by broadcasting quality programs and education. It is clear that PBS is on the continuum of "the journalism of enlightenment," which is accompanied by a reformative political view. In fact, the way that *Battle for Korea* describes history is consistent with the epistemology of the Great Man theory of history. Every critical turning point during the Korean War is explained as coming from an individual politician's decision. For example, the voice-over narration explains that the Korean War began because an ambitious Kim Il Sung sent army troops across the border. In the same manner, many historical moments in the narration are described with reductive statements, such as: "Mao decided to defeat the Americans in order to protect communism in Asia"; "Stalin joined allies against Japan"; and "Truman offered Stalin the 38th parallel." Such a Great Man theory of history, which illuminates the track of politicians' power rather than the socioeconomic context, has the potential to blind us to the complicated layers of history that exist below the surface. This approach is particularly problematic in remembering the Korean War because, as many historians argue, the domestic class conflict developed under Japanese colonialism was one of the critical causes of the war.[46]

As a more detailed background for the war, from 1910 to 1918 the Japanese colonial power had a land registration law that clarified the ownership of Korean land. In this comprehensive land survey process, Korean peasants were largely dispossessed because of their ignorance of the law and because of the colonial government's willful misinformation.[47] As a result, right before the liberation, Japanese officials and Korean landlords controlled most of the land in Korea. This imbalance in land ownership created extremely wretched living conditions for the majority of Koreans. Cumings states that even moderate historians would agree that the land issue in Korea was "hopeless without radical change."[48] Such exploitative economic conditions had continuously aggravated political tensions.

Between 1945 and 1950, Korea had been extremely polarized between the right and the left, and had already experienced internal warfare. Before the Korean War, considerable casualties had occurred due to increased guerrilla activity in the Jeolla provinces, the revolt of Yeosu and the Cheju Island Rebellion.[49]

As noted above, the issue of social class is surely a key factor in understanding the war. Yet *Battle for Korea* frames the Korean War as a battle of the Western powers after the Second World War, in which America is surely the protagonist. In other words, the film greatly highlights the international power relations in the context of the Cold War, yet largely ignores the domestic context of the Korean Peninsula. Looking at the history with classless lenses, *Battle for Korea* fails to represent fairly some significant moments of the war. For example, there are some scenes that portray workers demonstrating on a street in South Korea. These scenes are not used to explain the internal class struggle prevailing in Korea, but rather to convey the influence of communism on Korea before and during the war. Instead of enhancing the context, the film translates nearly every image of the people's resistance with rash value judgments, such as referring to their struggle as "Communist infiltration." As another example, the harsh guerrilla fighting against the South Korean government is described in this way: "To undermine the southern government, Kim sent his army raiding across the border. He armed and trained 20,000 guerrillas and sent them south to join southern Communists already fighting inside the Republic. The winter of 1948 and early 1949 saw intense fighting all over South Korea. Towns fell into guerrillas' hands and were retaken, sometimes brutally, by southern government forces. Some southern units mutinied and joined the guerrillas" (*Battle for Korea* narration). Through this narration, viewers may form the idea that the force behind the guerrillas was communism, while not getting answers to these crucial questions: Who are the people called the Southern Communists? Why did they fight against their own government? Why did southern units mutiny and join the guerrillas? Moreover, the above narrative structure does not provide any room for the factual context of the guerrilla warfare in South Korea that has been uncovered by historians. Cumings reports, "The landlord took 30 percent of the tenant produce, but additional exactions, government taxes and various 'contributions,' ranged from 48 to 70 percent of the annual crop."[50] This stark picture of reality is not illuminated in the narrative content. Rather, in many ways, *Battle for Korea* echoes Eckert and his associates' criticism of American biases toward communism. They argue that "Americans have often tended to regard communism as a monolithic force centered in the Kremlin rather than as a congeries of localized nationalist and socialist movements with their own historical and cultural roots."[51] As a clear example, the U.S. media easily associate communism with negative forces. It is interesting to note that *Battle for Korea* employs a double standard in describing the Soviet control of North Korea and the United States' occupation of South Korea. While the Soviets appear as a threatening force against sovereignty, Americans appear as an indispensable aid that brings peace back to Korea. What is more problematic is that such a simplistic dichotomy has been delivered to viewers not in a tentative voice but rather in an assertive narrative tone.

While the analysis of the narrative structure of *Battle for Korea* shows how both narrative conventions and institutional ideology influence the ways in which a historical event is constructed, this highly constructed puzzle nonetheless has the appearance of a trustworthy historical account. This trustworthiness results not only because the applied narrative techniques—the dogmatic voice, the chronological causality, and the ambiguous structure—enhance illusory authority in the representation of history documentary, but also because PBS appears as a channel with cultural authority for disseminating historical and cultural knowledge to viewers. These factors require that both historians and communication scholars critically deconstruct historical texts that the media structure and circulate, in order to motivate viewers to resist the illusory legitimacy that media institutions hold in telling history as well as to encourage viewers to find possible counter-narratives embraced in archives from the past.

When this textual analysis of *Battle for Korea* was conducted, U.S. military measures were taking place in Iraq whose context again was called a "war." Certainly the mass media showed an omnipresent power in developing images of this historical moment. The broadcasting industry landed in the battle arena just after the first troops; with advanced camera techniques, they collected many kinds of visual documents, stored them in a warehouse, quickly constructed provocative visual products, and disseminated those products through pervasive channels. Someday they will conduct another critical mission that reconstructs the meaning of visual archives, in which collective memory will be shaped and history will be told.

Battle for Korea, a historical documentary made five decades after the Korean War, is an exemplary case that shows how the media have increasingly been involved in an act of remembering: selectively absorbing and constructing newly found archives that have the potential to bridge our present and our past. Like any other memory acts, the media's performance in remembrance can either strengthen or rupture dominant narratives about past events. The potential that media have as vessels of subversive memory draws our attention to the possibility of the historical documentary as a site of struggle in which heterogeneous remembrances continuously merge as well as clash in the process of narrative construction.

Despite a rich collection of newly unearthed visual documents, *Battle for Korea,* however, does not succeed in substantiating the positive view of historical documentary as a dynamic site of memory, nor does it encourage viewers to participate in a discourse in which counter-narratives of the war can arise. Rather, an analysis of this documentary suggests a reductive treatment of a war that one might argue is one of the most complex subjects in the area of representation. Such a reductive treatment of the Korean War takes place at two levels: first, in the film's visual structure through its decontextualization of historical archives, its highly selective exposure of images to accommodate given narratives, and its modest effort at being reflexive; and second, in the film's narrative structure through its use of a univocal voice of "God," its causal explanation, and finally the conservative interpretation that emerges from its discursive and institutional context.

In conclusion, the analysis of the film *Battle for Korea* reveals that the conventional form of historical documentary is too monolithic to create a holistic lens through which viewers can be exposed to history's nuance and complexity. The mainstream compilation documentary is more likely to reinforce given narratives rather than rupture them because its audiovisual conventions block archives, whether or not they have been recently unearthed, from being connected to counter-voices. Thus, a historical documentary that utilizes conventional techniques has the potential to become part of an official culture in which the narratives of the past promote the consensual sense of "what the past should be like" as opposed to "what it feels like."[52] This film warrants concern among memory scholars that mass media can be conservative memory vessels that numb viewers' negotiating power against official narratives.

Most important of all, as both Barthes and memory scholars contend, *Battle for Korea* illustrates that the utterances of archival images—exposing the facets of a complex reality that can hardly be wrapped in simplified and plausible narratives—can become weakened and even sterilized within a discursive and institutional context. Constrained by the Cold War ideology that still substantially shapes American popular perception of the war, *Battle for Korea,* despite its rich historical materials, portrays a conservative reconstruction of the Korean War. Nonetheless, such a conservative bias of the film was diffuse, if not invisible, because of the rhetorical ambiguity that historical documentaries often build up in order to appeal to everyone, regardless of their point of view. This factor calls for more thorough and careful attention from communication scholars to media's increasingly sophisticated, yet often problematic role in reconstructing past events. It is the hope here that this analysis of *Battle for Korea* will encourage both scholars and viewers to look at historical texts regarding the Korean War more critically. In particular, an evolving context of the memory of the Korean War requires more vigilance to discern whether counter-memories that have emerged from the newly found archives (i.e., the new history) are anchored by uncontested narratives nurtured by ideological frames (i.e., the old present).

CHAPTER 4

"Mythologizing" Memories

A Critique of the Utah Korean War Memorial

It was serendipitous that I came upon the Utah Korean War Memorial in the summer of 2006. As a newcomer to Utah, I had been randomly exploring the historic sites of Salt Lake City. One day I found a site called Memory Grove Park in the vicinity of downtown. The park was impressively serene, with well-maintained vegetation and historic decor. I would have been just one of the many mindless strollers if I hadn't accidentally found a V-shaped, somewhat gaudy and fresh-looking memorial that stood out against the archaic backdrop of the park. To my surprise, this nascent mnemonic object was dedicated to the Korean War. At first sight, as one who had originally come from the Korean Peninsula, where the memories of the Korean War are far from consensual or stagnant, I immediately experienced an affinity for the memorial.

Soon after I commenced a case study of this memorial, I learned that the Utah Korean War Memorial—unlike the national memorials on the National Mall in Washington, D.C.—did not have its own official records of birth history; with the exception of a couple of articles in local newspapers, few written documents about it existed. To trace the memorial's unnoted history, I therefore began to track down the people who had been involved in the construction of the memorial, including veterans, a designer, and a city officer.[1] They provided me with compelling testimonies as well as invaluable memorabilia (notes, drawings, photos, letters, and so forth), all of which greatly sensitized me to the meanings of the memorial in the specific context of the space and time of its construction.

The Utah Korean War Memorial came to exist in 2003 when the United States unprecedentedly boosted American memories of the Korean War at its fiftieth anniversary.[2] The passage of fifty years had transformed the young soldiers who had gone to the battlefield in their late teens and early twenties into old veterans who lived their daily lives with a heightened sense of the brevity of the human life span. Thus, the timing of the fiftieth anniversary seemed to effectively mobilize veterans to participate in commemorative events at local sites. Many joined in the building of memorials in their home cities across the United States, including Wichita, Atlantic City, Philadelphia, and so forth. Echoing the nation's belated memory boom of the forgotten war, Utah Korean War veterans in 2003 erected a memorial at Salt Lake City's Memory Grove Park, one of the region's most respected secular commemorative sites.

Local commemorations of the fiftieth anniversary of the Korean War, encouraged by the U.S. Department of Defense during the years from 2000 through 2003, provided Korean War veterans with a rare opportunity to attempt to make their memories comprehensible to the public. Given the context of the U.S. collective memories of the Korean War, in which forgetting supersedes remembering, local veterans seem to have long yearned for public attention to be focused on their sacrifices on the unknown battlefields of Korea. Korean War veterans thus seem particularly vulnerable to the process of depoliticizing memories. In this milieu, the present case study of the Utah Korean War Memorial provides an analytical lens through which the audience is able to critically appreciate the broader phenomenon of memorialization of the Korean War that has recently taken place in towns and cities across the United States, reflecting in particular America's commemorative spirit for the war's fiftieth anniversary. More specifically, Utah's memorial resonates with three mythical scripts—*resilience, local pride,* and *the good war*—that emerged from both local and national contexts of remembering. This case study reveals how such scripts have allowed veterans to negotiate tensions between the individual memories that evolved from their firsthand experiences of the war and the official narratives that emerged from the U.S. collective memories of the Korean War; this research also explores how the official commemoration of the war has shifted local veterans' rhetorical positions from those of potentially subversive witnesses of the peculiar realities of the Korean War to those of uncritical negotiators who translate local experiences to national topoi. In this shift, veterans' authority in telling about the war has been appropriated in order to naturalize the very process of mythologizing memories; in this process, such appropriation ultimately has alienated them from their own experiences during and after the war.

It has been noted that the meanings of war memorials are subject to numerous factors, such as war realities, political narratives, memorials' materiality and aesthetics, the context of time and space, and viewers' perspectives. Thus, war memorials tend to communicate ambivalent meanings and often trigger conflicting messages in the public's mind. Memorials in towns and cities can be even more complex, since they convey local sentiments that may not be identical to the national ethos.[3] In the case of the Utah Korean War Memorial, however, such a polysemous quality of memorials seems to have been undermined by what has been distinctive about the U.S. collective memories of the Korean War. In the United States, the Korean War has been forgotten, uncontested, or, more bluntly, "orphaned by history."[4] The question of why the war has been forgotten can invite many plausible speculations: the unclear ending of the war, its sandwiched timing of occurrence between two major wars, its unpopularity in the mass media, the constraint of Cold War ideology, and the closed dialogues between South and North Korea. Without contemplating such a forgotten nature of the war, however, the United States commemorated the fiftieth anniversary of the Korean War by repeatedly highlighting the mythical narratives surrounding the war. In this milieu, an intensive case study of local memorialization is critical, since it illuminates how the national meanings of the Korean War have been constructed, reaffirmed, and contested through the history of local memorials.

Memory is not merely an abstract image of the past, but also a frame that provides us with a way of constituting the past with the perspective of the present. In his book *On Collective Memory*, Maurice Halbwachs articulates how the social framework of memory takes place in relations between collective and individual memories. He reminds us that although collective memories are formed within a group and gain strength from a particular body of people, "it is individuals as group members who remember."[5] Halbwachs also stresses that although collective memories provide the script by which individual memories are guided, the relationship between collective memory and individual memory is not one-dimensional but rather dialectic: "These two memories are often intermingled. In particular, the individual memory, in order to corroborate and make precise and even to cover the gaps in its remembrances, relies upon, relocates itself within, [and] momentarily merges with, the collective memory. Nonetheless, it still goes its own way, gradually assimilating any acquired deposits. The collective memory, for its part, encompasses the individual memories while remaining distinct from them. It evolves according to its own laws, and any individual remembrances that may penetrate are transformed within a totality having no personal consciousness."[6]

Halbwachs' description works on two notions: the totality of collective memory and the autonomy of individual memory. Collective memory achieves what Althusser calls the "material stance" of superstructure that ultimately alienates individuals whose acts of remembering compose its very totality.[7] Put another way, collective memory becomes an ideological apparatus by which individual memories are located as well as decontextualized by predominant thoughts of the past. One might argue that the more essential feature of collective memory, however, resides in its conflicts with individual memory. Consequentially, the autonomy of individual memories may endow collective memory with a less stable as well as a more dynamic totality than other social entities embrace.

The notion that totality has a bud for subversion has intrigued many scholars to distinguish collective memory from history.[8] While history presents a neatly packaged version of past events, memory foregrounds an untidy process in which a mythical narrative is constantly negotiated in the dialectic relationship between individual and collective memories. The process of mythologizing memories enables individuals to make sense of their experiences in an attempt to identify their relation to collective memories. Simultaneously, it also allows the collective memory to legitimize (authenticate) itself with the very evidence (probability) that it can locate individual memories within its script.

Mythologized memories are particularly palpable in war commemorations. Scholars who have critiqued World War II memories in both Russia and America have shared the notion that war memories are highly instrumental in forging national myths, narratives, and identities.[9] As shown by the controversy surrounding the *Enola Gay* exhibit at the Smithsonian's National Air and Space Museum in 1995, any attempts to problematize given narratives in hegemony often trigger formidable resistance from the status quo.[10] Facilitating such politicizing memories, the World War II memorial was dedicated at Washington, D.C., in 2004 with the aim of "[upholding] myths of national power and innocence that have long been central to America's collective identity."[11] Given this milieu, the U.S. popular culture also has glorified World War II veterans as "the Greatest Generation," whose members are selfless, brave, dedicated, and patriotic.[12] Similarly, Russian literature, spun through Soviet propaganda, has been highly saturated with the heroification of World War II soldiers as the Red Army: strong, farsighted, and cause-oriented.[13] Still, whether codified in official commemoration or in the culture industry, collective memory cannot be formed without individual memories. It is thus not uncommon for veterans to play a substantial role in constructing war myths through their participations in witnesses, reenactments, and rituals. In search of higher meanings (camaraderie, manhood, and patriotism), individual soldiers even voluntarily craft sagas, the myths that make their realities easier to bear.[14]

In his book *Remembering War,* Jay Winter offers the thoughtful insight that veterans' locations as rhetors vacillate between topoi and experience. Bearing witness to a war is an elusive task because it is "an effort to think publicly about painful issues in the past, an effort which is bound to fade over time."[15] Soldiers remember, speak, and forget, oscillating between the past, where their experiences momentarily took place, and the present, where their memories are constantly reconstructed. Thus, their acts of witnessing are inevitably caught up in power relations between the past and the present, specifically the present's attempt to reconstruct the past with a contrived narrative to accommodate a given ideology[16] and the past's persistence in constraining such selections of memories in the present with a set of factual substances.[17] One facilitates myth-making, and the other myth-breaking. To understand how Korean War veterans strive to situate themselves in this ongoing tension between the past and the present, one needs to locate their memories within the larger context of both national and local remembrance of the Korean War.

AN UNCONTESTED WAR

To the American public of the 1950s, a war that was fought thousands of miles from home seemed to be as foreign as the location of the battlefield, the country of Korea itself. Moreover, the cause of the war seemed to be clear neither to veterans on the front lines nor to their families at home. Even a father who found his son's name among the first reported U.S. casualties in Korea resigned himself to such remarks: "He was fighting against some kind of government."[18] When the war began, it was not even recognized as a war; rather it was called a "police action," an ad hoc term used by Harry Truman at a meeting with reporters to capture the meaning of a war that had begun without congressional approval.[19] Although the term "police action" hardly gives a sense of the magnitude of violence that took place during the war, the term "action" has long survived within American collective memories of the Korean War. There the war has been recalled only through an assertive, unambiguous framing: Communist atrocities were the cause, and the valorous action of the United States to rescue an endangered Korean Peninsula was the response.

Yet such an account seems to have much less to do with the battlefield realities of the Korean Peninsula than with the American political climate in the fifties, where McCarthyism relentlessly dismissed communism as "'un-American' and unworthy of legitimate consideration as alternatives to capitalism."[20] In fact, the outbreak of the Korean War "fully unleashed McCarthy and gave him a perfect soil," and in turn McCarthyism contributed immensely to politicizing the Korean War.[21] During the war, the prevailing abhorrence of communism called for an instant aversion toward Korean Communists, about whom the American public knew almost nothing. In their breaking news of the Korean War in 1950, Utah's flagship newspapers the *Salt Lake Tribune* and the *Deseret News* called one group of Koreans "Reds" and "Commies" who deserve American military's chastisement while generically calling the other "South Koreans." When the representatives of the United Nations came to Salt Lake City to enhance the public's support of the war, Utahns greeted them as forces fighting against "a grimly determined enemy 7,000 miles away": Communists in Asia.[22] As Amartya Sen notes, such a singular imposition of identity on unknown others seemed to have desensitized people to the magnitude of violence against their fellow humans.[23] Hardly any local news articles at the beginning of the 1950s questioned who these Asian Communists really were; few noted their aspiration for building an egalitarian society and for the removal of the colonial legacy in Korea.

Being remote from the battlefield context, people in America seemed to understand the war mostly in terms of its consequences for their own lives: its cost and its economic impact. To most U.S. citizens, the war was a vague endeavor that nonetheless demanded the recruitment of their young men from across the country. From Utah, 7,564 troops, either draftees or volunteers, went to Korea during the war, and 142 Utahns died in action.[24] Since the majority of Utah's population at the time was made up of the members of the Church of Jesus Christ of Latter-day Saints, the large scale of their draft challenged and limited the church's task of sending young members on their missionary journeys. In fact, the demands of the war contributed to a drastic drop in numbers of Latter-day Saints missionaries, from 4,847 in 1951 to 2,189 in 1953.[25] While removing young local people from their religious mission, the war nevertheless was a powerful stimulus to Utah's economy. During the war, the U.S. federal defense expenditure quadrupled, from about $13 billion in June 1950 to more than $50 billion by the end of 1951.[26] This increase greatly fortified Utah's defense industry, which had been developed mainly since World War II. Because of its location (equidistant from the main ports) and its climate (optimal for storage), the state housed substantial federal military installations, which not only brought new jobs but also facilitated the growth of local businesses.[27] An article on the front page of the *Deseret News* on August 17, 1950, reported: "Already, some 3,000 persons have been employed since the Korean outbreak," and called for more defense workers in Utah. Boosting the workload and employment in these installations, the Korean War helped Utah become one of the states that benefited the most from defense spending.[28] Thus, for Utah overall, the war imposed a demanding call upon its families and the local church, yet nonetheless strengthened an economic foundation that had existed since World War II.

Since the conclusion of the war, however, Utahns seem to have barely remembered the Korean War, a significant history that left a substantial impact on the present lives of much of their population. While other wars—World War I, World War II, and the Vietnam War—were commemorated with notable memorials in Memory Grove Park and on Capitol Hill, both of which are known as prestigious historical sites, the Korean War did not have its own publicly known commemorative site in the state of Utah until nearly five decades after its occurrence. Such oblivion within the community, which itself went unnoticed for far too long, must have defied the wishes of Utah's Korean War veterans, whose vivid memories are etched in their minds and on their bodies. Not surprisingly, many of these veterans, with the hope of traversing such long-lived forgetting, voluntarily participated in the erection of an overdue memorial in their home state. I found that the memorial that the veterans constructed largely resonates with three mythical narratives—*resilience, local pride,* and *the good war*—which emerged from both the local and the national contexts of space and time. In the following sections, I will discuss how each narrative has become a functional device through which veterans negotiate a tension between their own individual and the nation's collective memory in the process of mythologizing memories, and how this process has ultimately transformed a memorial into a screen that ideologically selects veterans' memories.

RESILIENCE

A city often has an archaic park that communicates its history and memory. As one of Utah's prestigious historic sites, Salt Lake City's Memory Grove Park is filled with mnemonic constructions, including the pioneer homes (1880s–1900s) that the Mormon settlers built to establish a lasting community. Over time, the park has offered both nurturing and healing. When the Mormon pioneers arrived in Salt Lake Valley in 1847 after a long journey in search of refuge, the park provided them with the necessities for survival in a new land: water to drink, irrigate crops, and power the mills, as well as lumber and stones to build homes.[29] During World War I, when mothers were deeply saddened by their sons' deaths on the battlefields of foreign lands, they came to the park and made symbolic graves for their lost loved ones. In 1924, the city dedicated the park as a tribute to Utah's war dead. Since then, the park has grown to be one of the state's most prestigious commemorative sites and has allowed Utahns—through a sense of local belonging—to transform individual sorrow and grief into collective mourning for their dead heroes.

Interestingly, the symbolic meanings of Memory Grove Park seem to have been strengthened by repeated natural disasters. In 1983, the snows melted off the mountains in springtime and flooded City Creek Canyon, where the park is located; the deluge poured through the streets of the downtown area. It is a well-known story in Utah that hundreds of volunteers quickly gathered and cheerfully constructed sandbag banks along the street to direct the waters onto safe paths.[30] Through subsequent years of renovation, the park was reborn with a much more controlled and organized appearance, leaving little evidence of the flood's devastation. In 1999, however, the park was badly damaged again, by a mammoth tornado that uprooted most of the mature trees and disheveled the landscape with muddy debris.[31] Again, a new blueprint of recovery for the park was developed. The city launched the Memory Grove Restoration Committee and the State of Utah designated a special financial budget to assist in rebuilding the park, a place that now embraces "significant historical and cultural value to the people of the state."[32]

Coincidentally, the city's aggressive recovery plan for the park was introduced at the same time that veterans in Utah received news that the Department of Defense was beginning to plan for commemoration of the fiftieth anniversary of the Korean War. This co-occurrence of events seemed to encourage Utah veterans to implement an idea that they had been talking about for a long time, but had never pushed for before. The idea was to erect a long-overdue memorial of the Korean War in Memory Grove Park. Members of both the Veterans of Foreign Wars and the Disabled American Veterans formed the Utah Korean War Memorial Committee and visited the city's Park Development Office to get an official

The Utah Korean War Memorial (Memorial Day, 2009)

endorsement for their mission. The city welcomed the idea and granted the group a small lot between the two memorials erected for World War I and World War II. The director of the Parks and Public Lands Division in Salt Lake City recalls: "It [the memorial] was initiated by veterans. . . . We [the city] provided them with only land, a piece of ground with a slab of concrete."[33]

While proceeding with their memorial project at Memory Grove Park, the Utah Korean War veterans experienced unusual attention paid to their memories of the Korean War through the nation's fiftieth anniversary commemoration. When I interviewed them, the veterans fondly recalled that they had been invited to various ceremonies marking the fiftieth anniversary and had been awarded honorary service medals. They seemed to appreciate receiving the attention at last, attention that they had not received five decades earlier. While returning veterans from the Vietnam War voiced their agonies and drew the public's attention to the war's true pictures in the 1970s and 1980s, most Korean War veterans returned home in silence during the 1950s with no welcoming parades. Utahn veterans whom I interviewed also recalled those moments: "When I came back from the Korean War, people did not even know I was gone. . . . They did not know where Korea was. . . . It hurt my feelings . . . and it still does today."[34] "Nobody even mentioned 'how did the war go?' 'what did you do over there?' ... so we just kind of turned off the emotions and shut down."[35] Such feelings of being unappreciated have been found to be universal among the Korean War veterans who related their stories in recently published testimonial books.[36] Not surprisingly, it was discovered that the term "forgotten war," a prevalent name for the Korean War in the United States, was initially coined by veterans who had found it difficult to communicate their memories to the rest of American society.[37]

Perhaps the absence of a memorial for their war had caused anxiety to aging veterans in Utah who longed for a more enduring memory vessel than their weakening bodies and minds. Perhaps, as surviving soldiers with a sense of indebtedness to their fallen comrades, they might have felt a special burden to communicate the untold memories that had never been brought to the public's attention. Thus, for these veterans, to build a memorial that would outlive their human life span seems to have been more than just an act of commemoration; rather, it was an act of releasing their burdens by laying their untold memories on a public shrine for future generations to witness. To ensure this legacy, between 2000 and 2003 half a dozen veterans in their late sixties and seventies worked vigorously to erect a memorial, by themselves at nearly every step of the way. This included working on the design,[38] raising funds, advertising, constructing the memorial, and acquiring engineering approval from the city.

What challenged these veterans the most was the fund-raising for the construction of the memorial, whose cost was estimated at between $75,000 and $100,000. Don Reaveley, a Korean War veteran and the chair of the Utah Korean War Memorial Committee, recalled the veterans' frustration when the committee's initial fund-raising efforts received only lukewarm responses from local businesses and potential donors. To overcome these financial obstacles, the committee advertised that donors of $100 and $500 would be recognized permanently on the memorial by having their names inscribed on the bronze wall and the granite wall, respectively. Although some criticism later emerged with the concern that the permanent presence of donors' names might undermine the integrity of the memorial, the committee believed that it was the only way they could persuade people to donate money to a local memorial for an unknown war. With persistence, the committee finally reached its fund-raising goal; the memorial was dedicated on July 27, 2003, in the midst of the nation's commemoration of the fiftieth anniversary of the end of the Korean War. It took nearly five decades for Utah's Korean War veterans to erect their own memorial in their home state. At the dedication ceremony, veterans declared: "Today marks the 50th anniversary of the signing of the armistice of the Korean War. Today, we will dedicate this memorial in honor of the 142 Utahans who gave the ultimate sacrifice for their God and Country. We must not and we will not forget their sacrifices. . . . They will no longer be forgotten."[39]

Since the summer of 2003, Utahns thus have had a more exhaustive site of war commemoration that displays memorials for World Wars I and II, the Korean War, and the Vietnam War; in addition they recently have begun to embrace individual monuments for soldiers who fell in Iraq. No matter how isolated and nuanced the feelings that the Korean War veterans might have held before, the newly erected Utah Korean War Memorial, along with the other monuments, has uniformly conveyed the theme of patriotism that transformed their long-neglected scarifications into memorable noble missions "for their God and Country." It is, however, disturbing that the tranquil scenery of the park, supported by meticulous maintenance, seems to have elevated the proofs of violence (killings and being killed) into honorable sagas of human history.

Interestingly, the narrative of Salt Lake City's Korean War Memorial parallels the primary theme of Memory Grove Park. Just as the city restored its historical park after repeated natural disasters and preserved it as a symbolic site that provides nurturing and rejuvenation to local communities of Utah, Korean War veterans in Utah determinedly preserved their fading memories against time and finally erected a memorial that resists public amnesia of their war. Such a parallel narrative of resilience seamlessly locates a new memorial in an old park. The benign amalgam, however, seems to have resulted in depoliticizing the memorial. Given the spirit of resilience, the memorial does not seem to provoke our lamentation over the massive violence nor any questioning of the causes for such loss. Rather, it suggests a conciliatory resolution that asks both mourners and questioners to move forward with a flow of habitual remembrances. In brief, the mythical script of resilience that is identified within the historical context of the local park has expedited the framework of memory whereby that script depoliticizes the rugged texture of individual memories of the war.

The signifiers of the Utah Korean War Memorial take multiple forms, including images, words, dimensional contours, and architectural displays. The two wings of the V-shaped black granite wall[40] simply display mnemonic fragments of the war. During my research, I found a dozen different drafts of conceptual designs from the files of the veterans, a city worker, and a designer. Although each draft has slightly different features and layouts, there nonetheless seems to be one central idea that persistently survived through the constant revising process of the design: to have the 142 names of the Utahn Korean War veterans who had been killed in action inscribed at the apex, the most central spot of the memorial. The completed memorial successfully carried out this idea.

One might wonder why the veterans were so determined to evoke the names of their fallen comrades. Interviews with veterans did not provide me with an immediate answer. Perhaps the veterans were attempting to search for higher meanings for their war experiences, such as the spirit of camaraderie.[41] Perhaps the names stand as a manifestation of the veterans' incommunicable experiences of the war.[42] Perhaps the inscription is meant more for the solace of surviving family members who will never be able to reconcile themselves to the abrupt separation between themselves and their loved ones.[43] The veterans' unyielding insistence on commemorating the names of the dead is subject to infinite speculation.

Although we cannot immediately fathom the inscribers' intentions, the abstract imagery of the names of the dead on a black granite wall evokes a sense of mourning for the loss. It also creates a momentary (if not elusive) montage, asking us to imagine the Korean War against the gloomy backdrop of the Vietnam War; just as the popular TV show *M*A*S*H*, set during the Korean War, became a successful allegory for an antiwar message against the Vietnam War. Indeed, in terms of civil strife, these two wars have much in common: the popularity of communism among the ordinary people, class conflicts in a local context, the inability to distinguish foes from friends, anti-Americanism, battlefields without a solid front line, and high casualties of both soldiers and civilians.[44]

Names on the apex of the Utah Korean War Memorial

Despite their intense experiences of such a guerrilla war, however, the Korean War veterans did not even have a proper term for their traumatic memories. American society accepted the notion of "post-traumatic stress disorder" as an official medical term only after the end of the Vietnam War.[45] Although their witness of the battlefield realities in Korea contributed to the cultivation of critical questions directed toward the subsequent Vietnam War of the 1960s and 1970s when history repeated itself in another Asian country, Korean War veterans themselves received little attention to their own suffering *after* the war. This particular context invites further speculations about what it means for veterans to name their dead. Perhaps the evocation of the dead comrades is a persistent call intended to draw public attention to the massive loss of their war. Perhaps it is an invitation to a belated welcoming parade that these veterans never received a half century earlier.

The meanings of the names can also be sought in the local context of war commemoration where listing the dead has long been the rhetorical cliché of war memorials. One may even suggest that nearly every local town in America has its own war memorials containing the inscription of names of dead soldiers who were born in that town. The names on a local memorial not only signify specific individuals whose deaths are grieved and whose stories are told by families and friends in town, but given the spirit of local patriotism, the names also stand as undeniable and proud evidence of the extent to which their community responded to the nation's call for sacrifice. Over time, such marks of community pride become a more critical function of memorials, since the populations of towns continue to change and become less well acquainted with the stories of individual soldiers. Ultimately, the names of soldiers function to negotiate a tension between local interest and national cause. Thus it is not surprising to find that the U.S. Army Office of Public Relations, during the Korean War, asked news reporters to find out *where the soldiers came from,* over and above the stories of who they were. An Army PR official remarked, "The importance of the individual in a news release from the fighting front should never be overlooked. Almost without exception, the people of the United States are interested in what the individual fighting man is going through in any action. In the individual, the people at home see themselves reflected. A soldier, sailor, airman or Marine does not have to be known personally for his words to carry weight. The mere fact that he comes from a particular town or state is sufficient to arouse local pride or interest."[46] Likewise, the Utah Korean War Memorial pronounces the names as representatives of Utahns, yet keeps the bearers of those names incognito to the public. Ultimately, the caption inscribed above the names puts the dead soldiers into a single category: *"Utah's 142 soldiers who paid the supreme sacrifice while defending their country under arms."* The political anonymity granted by the statement that every name represents countrymen who did their jobs for their nation has effectively embellished individual soldiers' deaths as a collective, prideful local response to the nation's call for sacrifice.

Such symbolic reduction can also be facilitated by the uniformed iconicity of names in memorials.[47] Regardless of their carriers' individualities, all the names of the Utah Korean War Memorial have a uniform look— white English letters against a black background. Given the conventions of naming, even the lengths of the lines are by and large consistent. The egalitarian look of the naming in the symbolic world, however, conceals the critical reality that these soldiers often came from the margins of society.[48] Don Reaveley, the chair of the Utah Korean War Memorial Committee, noted that seven of the names on the memorial represented individuals who came from Carbon County, a mining town where young people had few resources for achieving their dreams.

Initially, the committee identified 142 Utahns who had died in the Korean War by means of the Korean War Casualty File in the U.S. National Archives. After the completion of the memorial, however, three Utah families informed the committee that the names of their loved ones were missing from the memorial. After some investigation, the committee added these names. The number of the names on the memorial therefore has increased from 142 to 145. To veterans, it was a somehow expected change. In fact, the veterans who designed the memorial intentionally left room in the corner of the apex to include names that might have been missing from the official record. Ironically, the blank space waiting to be inscribed with hitherto unacknowledged and unidentified loss becomes a telling sign that evokes the frail memories of the Korean War.

THE GOOD WAR

As a domestically uncontested war whose battlefield realities were rarely exposed to the American public, the Korean War generated little myth of its own. Rather, it has been bequeathed much myth from World War II, a fight that is commemorated as "the good war" in American collective memories.[49] As Michael Adams has noted in his book *The Best War Ever*, the narrative of "the good war" also largely overlooks the complex realities of World War II: suffering, loss, failure, shame, and so forth.[50] Nevertheless, the Korean War and World War II cannot be regarded as similar combat situations, since they differ drastically in terms of scale, geography, political and cultural context, combat strategy, and local population. The strong association between these two wars derives from their historical proximity; the Korean War took place only five years after the end of World War II, and many veterans served in both wars. General MacArthur, an iconic figure of the Korean War, was also a protagonist in the memories of World War II. Moreover, before the completion of the memorial in Washington, D.C., in 1991, the primary national monument to the Korean War was the Tomb of the Unknown Soldier in Arlington National Cemetery that entombed unidentified soldiers from both the Korean War and World War II.

Although the link with World War II may have endowed the Korean War with more recognition and legitimacy in the minds of the public,[51] comparison with "the good war" represents an error of attribution that has been repeated in our act of remembering: to assign "a memory to the wrong source: mistaking fantasy for reality."[52] Such a misattribution has hardly encouraged the American public to be attentive to the specificities and particulars of the Korean War; rather, it promotes a willful forgetfulness, a decision to remember the war as vaguely as possible. As a result, American collective memories of the Korean War have left little room for critical questions: Why had communism become so popular in the Korean Peninsula right before the war broke out? Why did so many young, educated Koreans risk their lives against the U.S. troops? Why did most victims of both U.S. and South Korean troops feel compelled to keep silent about their suffering for more than five decades? In its failure to engage these critical questions, the Utah Memorial presents the Korean War with such habitual sound bites of war memorials as "sacrifice," "honor," and "freedom." These abstract words, devoid of local context, become void signifiers that resonate with little substantial meaning.

Besides the generic sound bites of war, a vagary of signification seems to persist even within the signs of specificities in the Utah memorial. For example, the right wing of the memorial shows a sizable map of the Korean Peninsula. At first sight, the map appears to be conspicuous because it foregrounds the image of Korea, in contrast to the generic war narratives of many memorials, which flatten the distinctiveness of individual wars. Unlike a usual map, this one highlights several areas of significance during the war, including the Chosin Reservoir, where more than 1,000 U.S. troops were killed in a battle with Chinese troops. The American public witnessed the repatriation of the remains of 19 U.S. soldiers from the Chosin Reservoir in 2004.[53] Even more than five decades after the end of the war, the land of the Korean Peninsula still exposes the vivid scars of the Korean War. An arbitrary line called the 38th parallel on the map has inhumanely separated families in the South and the North for more than half a century. Civilians above the 38th parallel are suffering from starvation that merciless human politics have aggravated. Barely evoking such enduring effects of the war, however, the memorial presents a nostalgic mimesis of a battlefield with neither scale nor

A panel of the Utah Korean War Memorial

geographic context. Under the spirit of the good war, the image of the map thus appears merely as the exotic shape of a foreign land for which American soldiers had to shed their blood in defending a vague notion of freedom.

Certainly the map speaks to the more complex realities of the battle-field when juxtaposed with veterans' individual memories. In my interviews with Utah Korean War veterans, they vividly recalled how the Korea Peninsula during the war was filled with destruction, devastation, and dehumanization. In addition to the deaths of their comrades, veterans also had to witness the unbearable sufferings of civilians: "What I saw was rubble, nothing . . . scattered people, frightened people, children who had no adults to be with them. It was just heartbreaking."[54] "What I did when I got back, after seeing so much destruction in Seoul, I took myself, my wife, and my young son and we went to New York City—just to see a city that hadn't been blown up."[55] "I felt sorry for them [the Koreans] . . . They worked hard to establish their little farms—they weren't big farms—and then have the military come and wipe them out, whether it was our military or the other military."[56] "Sometimes you'd see big mounds of white things laying next to the side of the road. You'd go up and look at it and it might be whole families frozen to death. That bothered me more than anything."[57] Interest-ingly, the veterans seemed to have offered the most concrete, intense, and highly empathetic testimonies when they recalled Korean civilians whose deaths during the war are counted at more than 2 million.

Despite its saliency in veterans' individual memories, however, the suffering of civilians is not explicitly acknowledged by the memorial. Rehearsing the official U.S. stance toward war commemorations, the Utah memorial consistently foregrounds soldiers as the sole protagonists. On the right side of the map, the memorial introduces a poem written by an unknown prisoner of the Korean War with the remark "In memory of those who did not return from POW camp #5—North Korea 1950–1953." We have little information about this POW poet who could not return home, and Clarence Peterson, the POW from Utah who introduced the poem to his fellow veterans, died before the completion of the memorial. Perhaps what makes the poem special is not its lines, but the fact that it was written by a POW. In American popular culture, POWs often appear as romanticized war heroes. Their stories are appealing because they highlight a contrast between foes with inhumanity and friends with valor—a dichotomy that can effectively codify any war as a good war. Likewise, this POW's poem inscribed on the Utah memorial strongly reinforces the idea of U.S. soldiers' noble mission for freedom in Korea by reminding us of the face of Communist captors whose malicious deeds (torture and brainwashing) are vividly imagined through popular culture.

Yet it is also important to note that the archetypal signification of the POW in American war commemoration blinds us to the peculiar pictures surrounding POWs in the Korean War. The official report indicates that there were 7,140 POWs during the Korean War. Of these, 4,418 returned home, 2,701 died, and 21 refused repatriation.[58] Unlike returned prisoners from other wars, returned POWs from the Korean War seem to have faced public skepticism about their exposure to Communist propaganda. As shown in the movie *The Manchurian Candidate* (1962), American popular culture has often portrayed surviving Korean War POWs as "brainwashed" or "turncoat" and thus invited public ignominy.[59] Such public skepticism has made most POWs from the Korean War reluctant to voice their experiences. Yet, without communicating any clues as to the peculiar trauma of Korean War prisoners, the poem on the Utah memorial is embellished with the slogan "Supreme Sacrifice" carved right above it. Repeating an error that assigns our memories to the wrong source, the poem evokes only a heroic image of the Korean War in the official codification of other wars.

Ultimately, the Korean War veterans I interviewed left me with a strong impression that they themselves proudly recalled their war as a good war. Certainly, the growth of both the economy and democracy in South Korea since the war seems to have convinced many veterans that the war was worth fighting. Three out of five veterans I interviewed told me that they had visited South Korea since the early 1990s and shared how amazed they were to witness the miraculous recovery of the Korean Peninsula from the total ashes of the battlefield. One veteran asserted, "If North Korea had won ... you would never have what you have over there [in South Korea] today." Another veteran willingly showed me a letter that he had received from South Korean president Kim Dae-Jung on the fiftieth anniversary of the Korean War. The letter begins with the following: "Dear Veteran; On the occasion of the 50th anniversary of the outbreak of the Korean War, I would like to offer you my deepest gratitude for your noble contribution to the efforts to safeguard the Republic of Korea and uphold liberal democracy around the world. At the same time, I remember with endless respect and affection those who sacrificed their lives for that cause."[60] The tone of the letter from South Korea is identical to that of the letter from the U.S. government marking the same occasion. The veterans I spoke with seemed to appreciate the official remarks that not only highlighted their forgotten war as a good war but also reminded them of the public's gratitude for their service.

Still, one should wonder how such official codification of the war has diminished the subversive power that veterans have in relation to the sites of memories. It encourages veterans to assign their memories to topoi in the present as opposed to their experiences in the past. It discourages veterans from witnessing the localities, specificities, and vivacities of the battlefield realities, all of which might deter the process of mythologizing memories. The good war narrative endows veterans with a rare opportunity to resurrect the memories of their war on good terms. However, it disturbingly transforms veterans' rhetorical positions from critical witnesses of the past into problematic facilitators of ideologically charged memory construction in the present. Such a transformation ultimately alienates veterans from their own memories, which never seem to be severed from the battlefield realities even with the long passage of time.

During my research, I encountered people who insisted that the Korean War had never been forgotten in America. As evidence, they pointed out that there exists a substantial volume of Korean War memory texts, including books, movies, and memorials. Yet few paid attention to the fact that many of these texts came into existence only within the last decade. Commemorating the fiftieth anniversary of the Korean War (between 2000 and 2003), America unprecedentedly engaged in the volatile act of remembering: honorary ceremonies for the Korean War veterans were held across the country, new memorials were built in local parks, unseen negatives of films formerly stored in the National Archives were developed for photo exhibitions, newly published books—memoirs, oral testimonies, military history—fattened the war sections of libraries, and a stamp featuring the Korean War Veterans Memorial in Washington, D.C., was issued by the United States Postal Service in 2003.

Echoing the nation's belated memory boom, the Utah Korean War Memorial was dedicated by local veterans on July 27, 2003, the day that the armistice was signed on the Korean Peninsula in 1953. Although I humbly admit that one cannot fathom the complex web of memories that have constantly been reconstructed in veterans' fading minds and bodies for more than five decades, I attempted to understand how veterans, through building a memorial, brought their untold memories to a public who hardly knew about the Korean War. I found that the memorial largely resonates with official tales—*resilience, local pride,* and *the good war,* all of which not only grip veterans' minds but also reside in the popular imagination of war. Emerging from the historical context of the local park, the tale of *resilience* celebrates veterans' persistent acts of remembering against both the passing of time and the force of public amnesia. Yet the theme also suggests a conciliatory resolution that encourages veterans to keep moving forward without voicing their own traumatic memories. The notion of *local pride,* embedded in the American vernacular commemorations of war, has transformed the names of the fallen soldiers from the intricate symbol of veterans' complicated memories into the banal token of a collective, prideful local response to nation's call for sacrifice. Finally, the mythical narrative of *the good war* that emerges from the association of the Korean War with World War II functions as an effective device through which veterans' visceral witnesses about the peculiar realities of the Korean War have largely been silenced. Veterans come to a site of official commemoration with alternating feelings of loss, guilt, redemption, pride, anger. Myths prevent veterans from losing themselves in the labyrinth of memory by informing them what to voice as well as what to silence.

Ultimately, the Utah Korean War Memorial communicates a patriotic ethos that reaffirms national values, identities, and narratives. Like numerous official memorials in America, the Utah memorial has effectively performed "the cultural work of turning the tragic aspects of war into honor and heroism and diminishing the reality of suffering."[61] What these patriotic memorials say to the public is the way wars should be remembered as opposed to the way wars might (could) be witnessed, recollected, and reconstructed; while these memorials tend to silence the visceral realities of the battlefield, the complex psyches of witnesses, and the incommunicability of trauma, they also tend to repeat the fairy-tale stories of good-will, valor, triumph, pride, and unity to accommodate the given ideology in a current political landscape.

Such patriotic memorialization predicts not only the type of war stories, but also the rhetorical positions of veterans who participate in this process. Given the historical context of U.S. collective memories, where the Korean War has been subject to more acts of forgetting than of remembering, Korean War veterans have, in particular, long yearned for public attention to their untold stories. Such a desire seems to have encouraged veterans to more willingly facilitate the framework of memory whereby mythical scripts of collective memories largely depoliticize individual memories. Ultimately, the official commemoration of the war has shifted local veterans' rhetorical positions. In recalling the battlefield realities, veterans were potentially subversive witnesses who deeply mourned the losses of both soldiers and civilians and critically testified to a gap between what they experienced and what society remembers about the war. As the creators of a memorial, however, the veterans became royal citizens who willingly translated their local experiences into national topoi. What is most disturbing is that this shift appropriates veterans' authority in telling the war in order to authenticate as well as naturalize the very process of mythologizing memories that alienates veterans' own experiences during and after the war. What this shift reflects is neither war realities nor veterans' memories, but rather a nation's willful forgetting of an inglorious past.

Finally, the Utah Korean War memorial reminds us that a war memorial does not always trigger our historical imagination of past event; rather, it can radically sever us from the visceral pictures of the war that enduring, living witnesses have drawn. A memorial that safeguards a society's ideals and values in the present thus tends to promote acts of forgetting, as opposed to acts of remembering. A memorial that ceases to question is no longer a mnemonic device in our symbolic world but an ossified relic of our landscape. Often a memorial outlives its creators. The rhetorical power of a memorial comes from inertia, a firm presence at a public place. Such inertia gains momentum over time with a memorial's acquisition of a historical look, which in turn authenticates the myths it embodies. Certainly the symbolic power of inertia will momentarily fulfill the Utah veterans' wishes that the durable existence of a memorial in black granite will prevent generations to come from forgetting the Korean War. However, we know that the durability of a sign also provides a necessary basis for an alteration in our symbolic world.[62] Perhaps the Utah Korean War Memorial will last long enough to be subjected to an alternative context where in which the meanings of the memorial will be questioned and where what had been lost in remembering will be sought again.

CHAPTER 5

"Shattering" Memories

The Statue of MacArthur in South Korea

Perhaps it was the end of the Cold War era that opened up the most intensive discussions about the iconic status that statues hold in our symbolic world. The news about the demise of communism in the former Soviet bloc often was conveyed via compelling images in which the statues of Lenin and Stalin were either destroyed by crowds or pulled down by new authorities. Occasionally, we were told about where these removed statues ended up: some, as commodities of nostalgia, were relocated to Soviet theme parks in former Communist countries; many others were recycled by monument factories in order to cast new ones for the new era; and still others were bought by travelers and displayed on the streets of America—sites devoid of context.[1] Such drastic transformations of Soviet statues seem to have inspired many scholars to ponder the ironic notion that a statue not only represents our efforts to perpetuate historical accounts, but also simultaneously reveals how transient those accounts are.[2]

More intriguing, there is strong evidence that mnemonic objects in public places can trigger contested meanings even without undergoing any physical alteration or displacement. Many studies on post-socialist change in Russia as well as in Eastern and Central Europe have illuminated how certain memorials and monuments survived the change of politics throughout history and how they have taken on new meanings that complicate, contest, or even reverse the originally intended meanings.[3] As the most striking example, Nina Tumarkin, in her book *The Living and the Dead,* introduced how the dissolution of the Soviet Union has transformed heroic statues of World War II—without any alteration—from symbolic icons of patriotic war to evokers of contested memories.[4] The insights of these scholars suggest that memorials and monuments are not mere signifiers of the status quo. As much as they have the capacity to crystallize narratives in hegemony within a current political context, memorials and monuments also have the unique rhetorical potency to trigger contested meanings in an era of political turbulence.

Supported by such scholarship, in this chapter I will elaborate upon the rhetoric of a statue through a case study of the MacArthur statue in South Korea. General Douglas MacArthur was the Supreme Commander of the United Nations forces during the Korean War. Since the war ended with an armistice in 1953, the iconicity of MacArthur has been a robust signifier that has communicated the dominant narrative of the Korean War: America rescued South Korea from malicious North Korean Communists. He has been remembered in particular as a hero in the saga of the amphibious Incheon Landing Operation on September 15, 1950, by which UN troops recaptured the capital of South Korea, cut off the North Korean troops' supply lines, and changed the course of the war that was nearly subject to a Communist victory. Commemorating this heroic saga, the South Korean government erected a statue of MacArthur in 1957 at Jayu (Freedom) Park in Incheon City. As a symbolic icon of both American benevolence and Korean veneration, this sacred image of MacArthur in Jayu Park has been revered in postwar South Korean society.

Yet memories, regardless of their forms, are subject to the ongoing reconstruction of historical narratives within a continuously evolving present context. In 2005, the statue of MacArthur at Incheon City was targeted frequently by iconoclastic actions. Reflecting the recent liberalized political atmosphere in South Korea that began to surface in the 1990s, many social activists and progressive historians have raised their voices to criticize both MacArthur's indiscriminate military actions and Koreans' uncritical perceptions of the U.S. role in the war. Given this context, these activists began to claim that the statue, an official codification that had been generating misunderstandings of the war, had to be either demolished or moved to a less prominent location. During the summer of 2005, leading up to September 15, which was the fifty-fifth anniversary of the Incheon Landing, tension around the statue had been intensifying: activists (unions, student organizations, dissident groups) frequently gathered to show their willingness to tear down the statue, while conservative groups (aged Korean War veterans, ex-marines, patriotic organizations) swore to protect the statue. These tensions culminated in a violent clash on September 11, 2005, during which hostility broke out among activists who were wielding long bamboo sticks (as part of their efforts to reach the statue), ex-marines, and police officers who were trying to maintain order around the statue. Despite such intensity, however, the 2005 protesters have never made any inroads into demolishing the statue, nor have they been able to move it to another location. The untarnished statue of General Douglas MacArthur still stands firm today in Jayu Park of Incheon City. Yet changes have occurred in the symbolic world. Through the 2005 iconoclastic actions, the statue of MacArthur has been transformed rhetorically from a reservoir of dogmatic memories to a site of contested memories where history is recalled through inconsistent, contradictory, and tentative narratives.

This case study of MacArthur's statue reveals two processes at work: first, how a statue, in a *time* of transition, transforms itself from a mere signifier of intransient history into a reflexive medium of transient memories of a past event; and second, how a statue, in its surrounding *space*, can embrace conflicting gestures that audiences from two different generational and ideological positions simultaneously perform. I argue that the subversive transformation of a statue is not accidental; rather it is predicated on a statue's unique rhetorical existence across time and space. I also argue that the new-media technology has amplified such a transformation not only because it can widely and promptly circulate the representations of counter-hegemonic actions (i.e., iconoclasm) but, more importantly, because it can permanently exhibit subversive audiovisual texts in a virtual space for public view. A statue, reconfigured in time and space, has the strong potential to become a dissenting medium that effectively reemerges subversive memories to confront consensual notions of a past event. To elaborate upon this notion, I will examine how a statue rhetorically functions in our symbolic world.

THE RHETORIC OF STATUE: CONTEXTUALIZING IN *TIME* AND *SPACE*

A statue is an iconic sign that mimics a real-life figure. We know that mimesis causes the reader's uncritical appreciation of what is signified.[5] Particularly, a statue increases the degree of mimesis by creating an effigy in a three-dimensional space where its relation to a reference (human body) appears to be "more direct and intimate than a painting's."[6] From the orthodox view of visual rhetoric, a statue appears as a conservative medium whose robust iconicity has the ability to crystallize, naturalize, and thus effectively communicate hegemonic messages without inviting much resistance from its audience. Yet the rhetorical characteristics of a statue can be much more complicated when we look at it as a medium that operates in the dynamic context of time and space.

The passage of time has significantly influenced memory construction since human bodies were deemed mortal, yet exclusive vehicles of memories. As Maurice Halbwachs has noted, while the limited human life span has deterred the endurance of memories, it has contributed to vivacity: a distinctive quality that memory has when compared to history.[7] With time, human beings have cultivated a variety of memory vehicles that have outlived the human life span. Accordingly, contemporary scholars have continued to study how such enduring memory vehicles have interacted with the passage of time in memory construction. Many have provided concrete evidence that historical sites which have lasted more than one generation tend to embrace contested meanings as new information and perspectives about the sites begin to emerge within a changing political and cultural context.[8]

Time particularly weighs on a statue because it is composed of imperishable materials, thereby creating immortal signifiers of human beings in our symbolic world. Cast in bronze or stone, a figural monument "alters the temporality associated with the person, bringing him into the realm of the timeless or the sacred, like an icon."[9] A statue thus bestows the illusive impression of immortality onto an historical figure whose legacy strongly lingers even after his or her death.[10] Like mimesis, this seemingly immutable permanence can also blind us to the constructed nature of a statue. As James Young warned, the "taciturn exterior" of a monument can become a mask of "the monument's inner life—the tempestuous social, political, and aesthetic forces."[11] Such an unchangeable facade of a sign seems to act in opposition to fluidity, a quality that distinguishes memories from history. Lasting monuments and memorials in public landscapes therefore can effectively trigger the myth of human experience as opposed to its realities.[12]

As is to be expected, there have been efforts to diffuse the reactionary impact that the endurance of mnemonic objects has brought to our symbolic word. Many artists have experimented with vanishing forms of sculpture in order to prevent a monolithic idea from being perpetuated during the countless reproductions of an unchanging object.[13] In the same vein, in commemoration of the Holocaust, young German artists created monuments that work against the rigid materiality of media: they introduced invisible, vanishing, negative forms of counter-monuments. Through this ironic form of memorial, these German artists wholeheartedly resisted the fascistic propensities of monuments to be authoritarian, didactic, and demagogical tendencies perpetuated by political powers.[14]

Yet there is a twist in our symbolic world. Despite these fascinating efforts to diffuse the endurance of materiality, I argue that a statue has the potential to be anti-fascistic, ironically because of the very permanence of the medium. Perhaps we can be reminded of the paradox of a sign that Ferdinand de Saussure points out in his semiotic tenets: "The sign is exposed to alteration because it perpetuates itself."[15] The idea that immutability becomes a condition for mutability has been hinted at in many scholars' insights on memory sites.[16] They have advanced an idea that the material endurance of a medium influences the way in which memorials and monuments rhetorically work within the sites of commemoration. The meanings of lasting mnemonic objects and places are constantly subject to their new, present surroundings of space and time. Often, in the present a caption that a creator (i.e., the older generation) once carved on the surface of a pedestal can conflict with newly emerging captions that appreciators (i.e., the newer generation) will bring to make sense of the statue in the future. At this moment of transition, a mimesis that has naturalized the creator's intention may no longer be potent in our symbolic interaction. In this case, durability transcends mimesis. The passage of time illuminates the dialogical quality of a sign in that meanings are constructed not solely through the features in a material form but also through the viewers' responses to them.[17]

Along with time, space also significantly shapes our rhetorical experiences within the sites of commemoration. While a spatial proximity contributes to the solidification and the maintenance of memories,[18] a place (a space with finitude) has strong mnemonic powers to trigger both public and personal memories.[19] Thus many scholars have noted political powers' attempts to ideologically control (organize) public space to privilege certain historical narratives.[20] As the most conspicuous effort to reinvent public space, a new regime often involves the (re)naming of historical streets, a symbolic action that introduces its ideology into the mundane spaces of everyday life.[21] Designating new names for old places can be "a censurable act of state-sponsored cultural silencing."[22]

Building a memorial is another common way of politicizing a public space. A memorial, "a social and physical arrangement of space and artifacts," (de)saturates meanings in political landscapes.[23] Uniquely, the fixity of a memorial creates a communal space wherein the audience experiences the presence of other visitors and witnesses their performances.[24] Often, what is taking place in such a communal space (who is visiting when) becomes more symbolically significant than any material objects filling up this space. Memory studies on postwar Germany have provided much evidence that memorials can create semiotic theaters where political leaders attempt to normalize the past through both the organization of ceremonies and the performance of particular gestures.[25]

Besides politicians, ordinary visitors also can bring symbolic meanings into space. As many witnessed at the Vietnam Veterans Memorial on the National Mall in Washington, viewers' spontaneous actions continuously negotiate, constitute, and counter meanings of the memorial.[26] More importantly, such audience gestures on the spot are often captured in a variety of representations, become embodied iconicity of the memorial in our symbolic world, and influence the ways in which we make sense of the memorial. At this moment of representation when the audience's bodies are incorporated into the scenes of a memorial, "the public *becomes* the sculpture."[27] Without space, such a moment would not be possible. Likewise, an inert existence of a statue in a public location creates a subversive room where the public brings unpredictable audiovisual elements that can both reinforce and rupture meanings that the very iconicity of a statue provokes.

Looking at a statue in the context of both time and space may remind us of a ritual view of communication, a notion that James Carey eloquently elaborates in his book *Communication as Culture*.[28] He argues that communication is not merely the act of transmitting information, but rather the process of constructing realities by which one can actively participate in reinforcing given meanings, in maintaining shared beliefs, and in engaging in alternative realities. Carey's view reinforces our attention not only to what the iconicity of a statue signifies, but also, and more importantly, to what takes place surrounding the statue: both hegemonic and counter-hegemonic actions. As an example of hegemonic actions, a statue often becomes a centrifugal location for ritualistic ceremonies— *media events,* as Dayan and Katz would term them—that celebrate reverence, reconciliation, and royalty within a larger community.[29] Contrarily, a statue also can trigger counter-hegemonic actions—*image events,* as DeLuca and Peeples noted—that exalt violence, confrontation, and disobedience in the public's eyes.[30]

To elaborate further upon the rhetoric of a statue, I will introduce a case study of the statue of MacArthur in South Korea, a country that has undergone a drastic memory transformation in its recent liberal political atmosphere. In what follows, I will first contextualize the iconicity of General Douglas MacArthur within the mainstream commemoration of the war. I will then discuss how this arbitrary linkage between the signifier (the iconicity of MacArthur) and the signified (the official narrative of the war) has been contested within the rapidly evolving context of memories in South Korea. This case study will ask us to look at not only how a statue over time transforms itself from a mere signifier of intransient history into a reflexive medium of transient memories of a past event, but also how a statue, with conflicting audience gestures in its surrounding space, can simultaneously embrace conflicting meanings that have emerged from two different generational and ideological positions.

In 1957,[31] Syngman Rhee, the first president of the Republic of Korea, erected the statue of MacArthur in the Foreign Park to remind the public of the nation's gratitude toward this U.S. general's legendary action. Since then, the name of the park has been changed to Jayu (Freedom), signaling a message that "freedom was restored owing to the success of Incheon Landing Operations."[32] President Rhee came to power in South Korea in 1948, with the support of the U.S. military government. As a strong adherent of anti-communism, he was extremely hostile toward communistic ideas, to the point that right before the Korean War, American advisers in Seoul argued for "limiting the types of weapons provided lest an overconfident President Rhee invade the north."[33] The erection of the statue therefore could be viewed as a symbolic gesture on the part of South Korea that reflected not only Rhee's political aspirations to build on his ties with the United States, but also his intention to legitimize hostile policies against communism in the Korean Peninsula. Rhee's regime publicly announced the conception of the statue, sent an invitation to MacArthur to come to the ceremony, and widely raised funds from the South Korean people.[34] The words inscribed on a stone in front of the statue could not reflect Rhee's political ideology more clearly:

> There is no boundary in justice nor is there any obstacle to struggle, mountain or sea. A man who executed such a struggle in the spirit of justice. . . . It was here at Inchon that we knew the incaloulable [incalculable] height of his genius. With the infinite capacity of his vision he conceived, and on September 15, 1950, he personally executed an almost unbelievable landing operation which instantly turned the course of the war to the triumph of freedom and the salvation of this Republic. . . . We shall never forget what he and his valiant officers and men of the United Nations Command did here for us and for freedom. And until the last battle against the malignant infection of communism has finally been won may we never forget it was also he who said. "In war, there is no substitute for victory." (Words inscribed on the stone base)

Anyone who reads this statement has to step back in order to view the actual statue that is mounted on an elevated pedestal. The prominent location of the statue high above the ground creates a significant distance between viewers and the statue, "a sacred zone" that brings a sense of awe to one's viewing experience.[35] This fifteen-foot-tall bronze effigy of MacArthur, mounted on a stone base, looks farther to the Sea of West, an ocean that meets the port of Incheon. His right arm is holding a pair of binoculars that evokes the moment of Incheon landing when MacArthur put his vigilant eyes behind the binoculars as his ship approached the first landing site, the Green Beach of Wolmi Island. His left arm, as if it were a lever for his vigilant body, is firmly placed behind his back. His profile exposes a sharp nose, which not only is an immediate signifier of his being a Westerner, but also is an evocation of his air of confidence, because in Korea one who has extremely high self-esteem is referred to as having "the high ridge of the nose." The statue in South Korea strongly echoes the U.S. public memories of MacArthur: a charismatic general who had both grandiloquent oratory and indomitable presence in public arenas.[36]

In the United States, MacArthur has been commemorated through a variety of forms of memorials, including the MacArthur Memorial Museum in Norfolk, Virginia; MacArthur Drive in Arlington National Cemetery; and MacArthur Park in Los Angeles. Although MacArthur was a controversial figure in U.S. history and was even dismissed by President Truman in the midst of the Korean War due to his insubordination in a changing political climate,[37] he nonetheless has been remembered in U.S. public commemorations as one of the greatest war heroes. Even upon his return home after the president's dismissal, he was ardently welcomed with a public parade. This zealous reception contrasted with a reality in which ordinary soldiers returning from the battlefield of Korea were met only with public ignorance and silence. The heroic image of MacArthur in the United States, which defies the historical controversy about him, seems to be a result of both his fame during World War II and his subsequent heroification in the official commemoration of that war: "The museum perfected an imperfect man."[38]

Heroification in collective memories can take various forms and nuances depending on the cultural, political, and historical context.[39] Overall, statues in Korea have been recognized as sacred objects. In the

A statue of General Douglas MacArthur at Freedom Park, Incheon

custom of shamanism, people have worshipped various forms of three-dimensional objects, including stones and trees, as hallowed icons of unknown gods. Furthermore, since the fourth century, when Korea adopted Buddhism from China, Korean people have been acquainted with godly statues in the form of bronze or stone effigies of Buddha in sacred temples.

While statues in the former Soviet bloc grew out of an Eastern Orthodox tradition in which an iconic sign is not a mere representation but rather "the incarnation of holiness,"[40] statues in Korea have been viewed similarly with a sense of awe, linked both to the tradition of Buddhism and to the customs of shamanism. In this context, Rhee's political codification of MacArthur in the 1950s seemed to achieve great success. Even demonstrators against Rhee's dictatorship in the 1960s left flowers in front of the MacArthur statue to express their gratitude, and there were shamans in South Korea who believed in the God of MacArthur.[41]

Over time, however, the iconicity of MacArthur has ceased to be considered as a mere signifier that enables the authoritative regimes of South Korea to promote the notions of both anti-communism and the United States–Republic of Korea alliance. The durability of bronze has preserved the physical reality of the statue for more than half a century, during which time it inevitably has interacted with newly emerging narratives of history in our symbolic world. Although many South Koreans, like the Filipinos and the Japanese, still have been willing to pay deep homage to this foreign general who they believed provided gracious protection from the North Korean troops, they cannot help but witness the emerging counter-memories within the evolving contexts of politics, culture, and demography. In brief, the statue has been subject to a choreography of history and memory and in the process has manifested the transience of the past in our acts of remembering.

A CONTESTED HERO IN A NEW CONTEXT OF MEMORIES

Since the spring of 2005, activists occasionally have gathered around the statue in Freedom Park and demonstrated their desire to demolish it. These protests provoked another group to be present in the park. Aged Korean War veterans (mostly ex-marines), who had publicly sworn to protect the statue from any iconoclastic actions, surrounded the monument at these times. Riot police also were present, not only to protect the statue but also to keep order between those who wished to demolish the statue and those who wanted it to survive. Tensions mounted in Freedom Park, culminating on September 11, 2005, four days before the fifty-fifth anniversary of MacArthur's landing at Incheon, when about four thousand demonstrators armed with metal pipes and bamboo sticks attempted to tear down the statue. Collision between demonstrators and police officers seemed to be inevitable, and subsequently there were wounded participants on both sides. Not surprisingly, such turbulent actions around the statue drew intense media attention. A variety of news media, including television networks, newspapers, the Internet reports, and radio programs, captured and disseminated provocative images and words, poignant by-products of iconoclastic actions.

Feeding media with incendiary sound bites, many progressive civic groups voiced their critiques of the Korean people's uncritical perceptions of both MacArthur's actions and the role of the United States during the Korean War. They claimed that U.S. troops were not liberators, but rather occupiers, who since 1945 had oppressed the Korean people's legitimate desire to build an independent country devoid of its colonial legacy. In their view, the statue of MacArthur was an imperialistic icon that needed to be removed not only from the physical public site, but from the public consciousness as well.[42] Some of the protesters even called MacArthur "a war criminal." As part of an effort to make sense of such provocative claims, the Korean media introduced a variety of remarks critiquing the roles that both MacArthur and the U.S. military government had played in the Korean Peninsula before and during the war. As the most subversive text, the following remark of Kang Jeong-Koo, a leftist sociology professor at Dongguk University, entered into the media sphere: "The Korean War was a civil conflict started by Kim Il-Sung for national unification. It would have ended in a month if American forces had not intervened. The statue of Gen. MacArthur, the war monger, should be thrown into the gutter of history. MacArthur is not a person who saved Korean lives, but an enemy who snatched away Korean lives. MacArthur was a war fanatic. The favorable perception of the war maniac who caused a great tragedy to the Korean people should be scrapped. His statue should also be destroyed."[43]

Regardless of the public's response and officialdom's backlash against Kang's account, the introduction of such a subversive voice into the legitimate media reflected the liberal atmosphere of South Korean politics that had begun to emerge since the beginning of the 1990s with the election of a democratic government for the first time since the end of the Korean War. This new political light unfolded a large body of counter-memories of the Korean War that had been suppressed under the military dictator-ships. As the best example, in 2003 South Korea's popular TV history pro-gram series *We Can Talk Now* (MBC) featured a surprisingly critical biog-raphy of MacArthur. The program presented American historian Michael Schaller's view that MacArthur regarded the Korean War as an opportu-nity to further his ambitions for the presidency. The program also made a case as to how his ambition prolonged the war that needlessly destroyed many lives, including those of Korean civilians and American soldiers, and how his obsession with victory may have resulted in an atomic bomb set off on the Korean Peninsula.

Furthermore, various channels of Korean media, mainstream as well as alternative, recently have begun to cover the problematic role that the U.S. military played during the Korean War. With the introduction of the arti-cles about the No Gun Ri killings and the Associated Press's 2001 Pulit-zer Prize award story, South Koreans become familiar with the subver-sive accounts of the Korean War that progressive historians persistently have conveyed but that were suppressed by official narratives.[44] Such accounts illuminate in particular civilian casualties that both the U.S. and the South Korean military troops inflicted during the war. Much of this commentary claims that the attacks by the U.S. Air Force, including the discharge of a myriad amount of napalm, resulted in the killing of count-less innocent South Koreans.[45] Correspondent Wilfred Burchett lamented that the United Nations, the world's most universal peace-keeping orga-nization, had destroyed almost everything that the North Korean people had inherited from their ancestors. Historian Bruce Cumings has gone so far as to call this a "genocidal war."[46]

Such an influx of new memories from "old history" in a time of political transition in South Korea has transformed the statue of MacArthur from a mere signifier of intransigent history into a reflexive medium of tran-sient memories in our symbolic world. The passage of time has changed the nature of space surrounding the statue. While the statue still functions as a magnetic location for old generations to practice hegemonic actions (i.e., reverence for the hero), it simultaneously provides a subversive space for new generations to perform their counter-hegemonic actions (i.e., downplaying the hero). In fact, the iconoclastic actions that took place against the statue of MacArthur in 2005 contributed to expediting the migration of counter-memories "out of the closets" of dissidents' dialogues and academic discourses into and onto highly accessible public sites. In the following section, I will discuss this paradoxical role that the statue of MacArthur has begun to play as a facilitator of both official memories and counter-memories of the Korean War.

CONSEQUENTIAL MONUMENT: THE REPRESENTATION OF ICONOCLASM

As many scholars witnessed during the collapse of the Communist statues, iconoclastic actions may result in symbolically formidable consequences in the context of both time and space. If actions actually remove a statue, such an event can be "a powerful interruption of the flow of time because of their intended durability."[47] Depriving a statue of its permanence and sacredness, iconoclasm unwraps the symbolic work of a statue: "The person it [the statue] symbolized dissolves into an ordinary, time-bound person."[48] Furthermore, actions ultimately can result in the erection of a new statue on the same space, which in fact happened many times in the former Soviet bloc. In this case, a statue functions as "a double semiotics" by becoming "the signifier of two signifieds: itself and what is absent, its demolished predecessor."[49] Yet iconoclastic actions do not always succeed in creating a stark visual signifier, either in the absence of an old statue or in the presence of a new one. Many actions, often deterred by the status quo, remained incomplete and subsequently disremembered by a seemingly untouched statue afterward.

Likewise, the statue of General Douglas MacArthur in South Korea remains untarnished. Without previous knowledge, a visitor to Freedom Park in Incheon City could hardly imagine any of the violent actions against the statue that occurred in September 2005. Somewhat ironically, after the turbulent season of those actions, the local government office of Incheon City thoroughly cleaned the statue for the first time in the forty-eight years since its completion. This historical cleaning has provided a new look to the statue, changing it from a greenish dark bronze to a yellowish bright effigy.[50] The flow of routine around the statue also has continued. One can still witness that South Korean citizens, especially those of the older generations, visit the statue and willingly express their gratitude toward MacArthur with

A South Korean Marine veteran at Freedom Park (November 25, 2008)

various types of gestures such as saluting, offering flowers, and pausing for pictures.

While visiting Freedom Park at Incheon in the autumn of 2008, three years after the iconoclastic actions, I accidentally witnessed an old gentleman who offered his salutation to MacArthur's statue. His salute lasted long enough so that I, an unprepared witness of this scene, could snatch a camera from my backpack and succeed in taking a picture of his back. The light from the sunrise resulted in an unintended silhouetted image that illuminates the solemn moment of reverence in the sacred space of the statue. In our brief conversation afterward, I learned that he was a South Korean Marine veteran who has been jogging in this park for the past three decades and has saluted the statue every morning as he passes it. Certainly, the statue unfailingly has provided this veteran with a safe zone in which he has continued to fulfill his daily routine of encountering his hero with the most respectful body gesture.

Yet we also know that the very space that graciously embraces this old man's royal gesture (i.e., a hegemonic action) allowed the acts of violence and confrontation toward the iconicity of the hero (i.e., counter-hegemonic actions) to take place in the public eye. Unlike the gestures of reverence, the iconoclastic actions are unfamiliar and provocative while abruptly interrupting the flow of routine. In many ways, the 2005 anti-MacArthur actions at Incheon in South Korea echo the 1999 protest activities surrounding the WTO Conference in Seattle in the United States. Activists in Seattle largely performed provocative actions (confrontation, agitation, and coercion), which in turn created compelling audiovisual texts for mass media dissemination. Unique at the time, this "unorthodox" rhetorical activity contested the hegemonic discourse surrounding the status quo via "critique through spectacle, not critique versus spectacle."[51]

Likewise, the images of 2005 iconoclastic actions against the statue of MacArthur were selling in the commercial media of South Korea not only because they possessed the spectacle of violence—"necessarily ingredients" for compelling viewers to watch[52]—but also because they contained extremely novel gestures toward the hero. The actions of confrontation and disobedience may have seemed astonishing to South Koreans who had been accustomed to seeing only gestures of reverence toward the statue of MacArthur. Contextualizing the sacred iconicity of the statue within chaotic motions, the images of iconoclasm thus have made the familiar statue unfamiliar. Furthermore, these rebellious actions around the statue have symbolically contested the arbitrary yet uncontested link between the signifier (the iconicity of MacArthur) and the signified (America as savior, deserving of Koreans' gratitude) within the official memories of the Korean War. Such subversive symbolic works can be further identified when one looks closely at visual cues within the images of iconoclasm.

In the process of photographing the 2005 protest surrounding the statue of MacArthur, many media practitioners in South Korea seemed to have chosen their positions behind the demonstrators, locations that allowed them to capture not only the dynamic vectors of conflict but also the statue itself that such conflicts targeted. As a result, many pictures that the media have introduced seem to have three distinct layers within the frames: (1) the demonstrators in the foreground, (2) the police in the middle ground, and (3) the statue of MacArthur in the background. While the statue in the distance appears to be static and tranquil, thereby evoking a sense of certainty and continuity, the mobile presence of demonstrators in the foreground unbalances that equilibrium by creating somewhat chaotic visual cues (unparalleled vertical lines of bamboo, inconsistent colors of outfits, and various heights and angles of postures). The police officers—symbolic icons of authoritative power with their uniformed outfits and movements—create a horizontal line, a seemingly impenetrable wall that divides the sacred zone of the statue from the zone of resistance. As the most intriguing visual cues, some of the demonstrators' long bamboo sticks appear to cross an impassable line in the picture. Although the sticks—unsophisticated armaments of the protestors— never reach the statue, their intrusiveness in the picture appears to create a subversive visual cue that symbolically undermines the unquestioned sense of awe and reverence surrounding the statue. Ironically, such pictures also have created a déjà vu kind of memory of the Korean War: that South Korean police before and during the war harshly oppressed those among their own citizens who raised any critical voices against the American military government.

These compelling yet illusive moments of iconoclasm have been vividly captured through various media of representation, including sound recorder, photograph, motion picture, and so forth. In the process, the mass media have immediately included a larger viewership in the spectacle of these fleeting iconoclastic actions, which otherwise would have been consumed solely by participants, authorities, and local viewers. Such mass circulation, however, is not the only collaboration that the media have made with the protestors of the 2005 iconoclastic actions. The modern media, equipped with digital technology, also have immortalized the illusive moments of protest that were halted by authorities in hegemony. Since 2005, the typing of the words "MacArthur Statue of South Korea" in search engines of either Google or Naver (the most popular Internet search site in South Korea) has brought up not only official or vernacular information about the statue of MacArthur at Incheon City, but also a variety of audiovisual texts expounding upon the 2005 iconoclastic actions against the statue. Through such collaboration with the media, the 2005 anti-MacArthur protest thus has created a lasting exhibition of counter-memories on virtual sites.

Certainly, the case of the MacArthur statue has reaffirmed the notion that the relationship between media and activism can be symbiotic. While activists provided media practitioners with compelling audiovisual texts of iconoclasm, media practitioners in turn have allowed their media to preserve as well as disseminate dissidents' critical messages. Furthermore, this symbiotic process has created unique by-products in our symbolic world: representations of iconoclasm. While actions are temporal, the representations of iconoclastic actions are permanent, leaving a lasting impact on our memories of a statue even after the statue disappears. As many witnessed the demise of the Cold War era in the former Soviet bloc, film technology has been able to immortalize "the moment of destruction, transforming it into its own brand of monument."[53] With digital technology, the durability of this new monument (i.e., the representation of iconoclasm) easily can surpass the life of a statue that is made of stone, bronze, or iron. What is more remarkable is that the iconicity of this new monument embodies not only the public's response to a statue but also the statue itself. Michael North's notion that "the public *becomes* the sculpture" therefore is manifested literally in this consequential monument of iconoclastic actions.

The case study of the statue of MacArthur has encouraged us to look at how a statue rhetorically functions in the dynamic contexts of *time* and *space*. With the durability of bronze, the statue has survived for more than half a century as a benign iconicity that evokes gratitude among South Koreans toward American benevolence during the Korean War. Such durability has provided the statue with a substantial life span that allows newer members of society in a transition of time to provoke questioning about the intended significations of the statue. With the emergence of counter-memories in such a liberalized political atmosphere, South Korean activists engaged drastic iconoclastic actions that called for either the destruction or the relocation of the statue. Activists failed to destroy the physical reality of the statue, yet nonetheless succeeded in shaking up the symbolic world within which the meanings of the statue are renegotiated. For future studies, I would like to examine the critical implications that this case study of MacArthur brings up about how the roles of public memorials can be in flux in the continual process of legitimizing the mythical ethos of a nation. In a way, a statue echoes the very constructed and incomplete nature of a nation. As a nation—itself a constructed entity based on historical and cultural myths—continuously (re)constructs the narrative of past events to accommodate ever-changing power relations, so too a statue—one of the popular national symbols—accordingly triggers alternating meanings of the past in public minds in the present.[54]

Like time, space also significantly weighs on a statue. Yet the relation between space and memory seems to have been only somewhat monolithically explored in the given scholarship of memory studies. For example, a confined space (spatial proximity), though not a prerequisite for building collectiveness, is considered to be an element that enhances the solidity as well as the intensity of collective memory. In particular, the attributes of a monument's relation to space—its fixity, inertia, and immobility— are deemed to be constituents that facilitate a consensual notion of the past among audiences who make pilgrimages to the site. The case study of MacArthur's statue in South Korea, however, has provoked us to look at the space surrounding the statue not only as a symbolic boundary that anchors our perception, but more importantly as a performative stage that invites the audience's actions toward a statue. Thus the space surrounding the statue may contribute to its subversive transformation in a time of transition by becoming a publicly open platform where audiences from different generational and ideological positions confront each other through conflicting gestures.

After all, a statue—reconfigured in time and space—has a strong potential to become a dissenting medium that triggers counter-memories against hegemonic narratives of the past event. Furthermore, I also argue that the potential of a statue to be a subversive medium has been increased with the introduction of new media. Nowadays, momentary gestures surrounding a statue can be captured immediately by digital recorders and displayed permanently on virtual sites for a larger spectatorship. Within this media milieu, the 2005 iconoclastic actions against the MacArthur statue in South Korea yielded a provocative representation of iconoclasm that has entered public Web sites. This consequential monument, which embraces the iconicity of the public's rebellious actions against a historical war hero, illuminates the paradox that a statue can be both a perpetuator of official memories and a facilitator of counter-memories in our acts of remembering.

For the first time since the war, the South Korean public has witnessed counter-memories squarely confronting the official narrative of the Korean

War at the wide-open public site of the statue. Subsequently, the constant display of audiovisual texts of iconoclasm at virtual sites has signaled a message that the imagining of a past event by means of solely one isolated account is impossible. While the untarnished statue of MacArthur (i.e., the old signifier) in a prestigious public park has continued to be present, evoking the official thesis of the war, a newly entered set of representations of iconoclasm (i.e., the new signifiers) has drawn the public's attention to the ongoing construction sites of memories where history is recalled through inconsistent, contradictory, and tentative narratives. The irony here is that such continual, open-ended reinterpretations of the past have been triggered by the long presence of a statue, a signifier that was initially meant to bring forth a closed history. From this new perspective, MacArthur's statue, once a signifier of intransigent history, now calls out to South Koreans to resist the grand narratives of official memories, to engage with the demystification of history, and ultimately to resist the absolute.

Epilogue

The close examination in this book of five memory sites in South Korea and the United States has revealed a somewhat kaleidoscopic image of how the Korean War has been subject to a variety of types of memory construction within the context of the fiftieth anniversary of the Korean War. Although the five sites are discrete, examined together, they have brought our attention to the recent surge of counter-memories that has significantly influenced the ways in which we remember the Korean War. With unprecedented scope and intensity, these counter-memories have brought us unknown stories, alternative frameworks, and detailed contexts that problematize the official narrative of the Korean War in hegemony. What has determined the viability of such counter-memories at each site appears to vary with the given narrative, ideological constraints, institutional forces, syntax of the genre, commemorative norms, and semiotic potency of the media involved.

For example, in the reconstruction of the No Gun Ri story, the U.S. media largely silenced subversive stories that emerged from the South

Korean survivors' testimonies, while constantly highlighting memories that tended to reaffirm the official narrative of the Korean War. As a result, the No Gun Ri story became sanitized and emerged as but another anecdotal war story that asks to be forgotten. As noted in the examination of the female narratives on the No Gun Ri killings, however, the survivors themselves also became conservative memory agents who voluntarily scripted stories that resonated with their given values. While the Confucian script of motherhood (mothers as reproducers, protectors, and expendable assistants of the male blood line) on the one hand enabled the No Gun Ri female rhetors to weave trauma into plausible stories, Confucian motherhood norms on the other hand provoked these women to reflect on their memories with a sense of culpability. Likewise, an analysis of the PBS documentary *Battle for Korea* reveals how Cold War ideology lingering in the U.S. collective memories of the Korean War constrained counter-narratives while perpetuating official ones. Yet, in the case of *Battle for Korea*, the film's conservative bias is diffuse, if not invisible, because of the rhetorical ambiguity that historical documentaries often build up so that they appeal to everyone, regardless of the various points of view among the audience.

Furthermore, it is noted that the potential emergence of counter-memories can be blocked by given norms that are largely practiced at the official sites of commemoration. As evidence of such blocking, the analysis of the Utah Korean War Memorial in Salt Lake City reveals how the official commemoration of the war shifted local veterans' rhetorical positions from potential witnesses of subversive realities of the war to uncritical negotiators whose legitimization of the very process of mythologizing memories ultimately has alienated them from their own experiences during and after the war. Ironically, however, the emergence of counter-memories also can be facilitated by the very medium that the official commemoration often has utilized. As an example of this, the case study of MacArthur's statue reveals how a statue, reconfigured in time and space, has the strong potential to become a dissenting medium that effectively reemerges subversive memories to confront consensual notions of a past event.

Such dynamic memory constructions witnessed at our five memory sites indicate that the Korean War, an event that recently underwent a semi-centennial anniversary, cannot be considered a closed history; rather, the war is still very much subject to the ongoing process of remembering in which untold memories are constantly introduced, manifested, and performed at various local sites. Granted that today's international politics about the Korean Peninsula are still volatile, the Korean War memories ought to be deemed invaluable sources from which one can identify critical frameworks for appreciating the complex power relations among nations in the present.

I completed my writings for this book in 2013 when we were bombarded with news about increasing tensions surrounding the Korean Peninsula. With its pronounced plans for nuclear testing, North Korea again has become the center of attention in our international community. The spotlight on North Korea regarding nuclear testing, however, was not an unfamiliar scene. What was unusual and thus worrisome about this time was that the audience had to witness a variety of drastic actions by different parties, all of whom obviously failed to facilitate official dialogue. Manifesting strong ties with South Korea, the United States sent an increasing number of troops, armaments, and facilities to the Korean Peninsula for military operational training with its South Korean counterparts. Meanwhile, North Korea continued to announce plans for a missile launch and even declared that it had nullified the 1953 armistice. As if war were imminent, media institutions in the West dispatched a number of reporters to South Korea, some of whom were quickly labeled "combat correspondents." The clear sign of an impasse came when South Korean workers returned home from Kaesong Industrial Park in North Korea, a facility that in the past has symbolized the two regimes' efforts for reconciliation and collaboration.

Such escalating tensions seemed to haunt us with a déjà vu kind of memory of the Korean War. In fact, media even weighed in with the fearful question of whether the built-up tension would result in renewing the war that had been halted six decades before. In the spring of 2013, memories of the Korean War seemed to hit many of us simultaneously, yet with starkly different images. At one point, a mainstream Korean newspaper[1] claimed that the U.S. military would bring in B-52s, strategic air bombers, for an operational exercise. The same article mentioned how this plan immediately provoked the North Koreans to reexperience traumatic memories of mass destruction caused by the Korean War. The article also cited the words of Kim Il Sung, the former leader of North Korea: "The U.S. air attack wiped out 73 cities in North Korea and only two buildings in Pyongang survived." This media story in turn reminds me of the artifacts of the Hill Air Force Museum at Salt Lake City, which I visited a few years ago. I saw an old body of a B-52, one of the significant historical relics that the museum displays to promote education about the history and mission of the United States Air Force. Surely, aircraft in the museum appear to be symbols of this nation's pride and its heroic efforts to keep the peace across the world. I recall innocuous scenes in which parents were taking pictures of their children as they interacted with the impressively huge body of the aircraft anchored on the ground. Such an antique look of a B-52 gracefully presented in a U.S. local museum did not hint at any clues that this very same mnemonic object could evoke the painful image of reckless violence in the north region of the Korean Peninsula.

Witnessing such fractures of remembrances, one might wonder whether memories can provide any viable frameworks through which we can appreciate the past. After all, memories are not representatives of what took place in the past. Rather, they are images of realities that we have continuously constructed, argued for, and dwelled upon in the process of negotiating the past in an ever-changing present context. Memories thus acutely inform us who we are now by foregrounding specific terms to which we in the present have tentatively arrived. We (individuals, communities, and nations) as agents of memories are on a ceaseless journey of searching for terms that not only will help us to negotiate the past but also will navigate us to move through the tangle of realities that we simultaneously construct in the present. Thus it might be fertile for future investigations to attempt to bridge memories that often are hopelessly fractured, divided, and even conflicted. Perhaps what we can and ought to do is to try to communicate memories as the complicated, inconsistent, and conflicting phenomena that they are. In the process, we might understand one another better by learning not only specific ideas that other parties have held about the past but more importantly why, how, and in what contexts they have come to such ideas in their acts of remembering. Memory matters—not because it approximates the past, but because it mirrors a process of who we are becoming in the present as well as in the future.

1. "SILENCING" MEMORIES

1. Charles J. Hanley, Sang-Hun Choe, and Martha Mendoza, *The Bridge at No Gun Ri: A Hidden Nightmare from the Korean War,* 269–81.

2. Sang-Hun Choe, Charles J. Hanley, and Martha Mendoza, "War's Hidden Chapter: Ex-GIs Tell AP of Korea Killing," Associated Press, September 29, 1999, http://www.pulitzer.org/works/2000-Investigative-Reporting.

3. Chung Eun-Yong collected testimonies from his wife that became an essential part of his book; then he waited to publish until the political atmosphere of South Korea had developed some tolerance for a story like No Gun Ri. The book, *Gdai, Wooriyi Apumyul Anunga?* [Do you know our pain?], is an autobiographical story in which his own and his wife's memories are seamlessly merged into a provocative testimony of the incident.

4. Jeremy Wagstaff, "Korea's New Crusaders."

5. I gathered the news articles by using the Internet search engine LexisNexis. To ensure a representative sample, I examined, with the guidance of *Time Almanac,* whether sampled articles from these online sources came from publicly recognized media institutions. The examination confirmed that all the selected newspaper articles ranked within *Time Almanac*'s 2004 Top 100 Daily Newspapers in the United States. Thus, articles from the following newspapers constitute the main body of text in this research: *USA Today, Wall Street Journal, New York Times, Los Angeles Times, Washington Post, New York Daily News, Chicago Tribune, Long Island Newsday, Houston Chronicle, San Francisco Chronicle, Chicago Sun-Times, Boston Globe, Philadelphia Inquirer, Atlanta Journal and Constitution, Cleveland Plain Dealer, Oregonian, San Diego Union-Tribune, St. Petersburg (FL) Times, Denver Post, Denver Rocky Mountain News, St. Louis Post-Dispatch, New Orleans Times-Picayune, Columbus Dispatch, Pittsburgh Post-Gazette, Milwaukee Journal Sentinel, Charlotte Observer, Seattle Times, Buffalo News, San Antonio Express-News, Omaha World Herald.* (The newspapers were displayed by rank in *Time Almanac.*)

6. Charles J. Hanley and Martha Mendoza, "The Bridge at No Gun Ri: Investigative Reporting, Hidden History, and Pulitzer Prize."

7. Vicki Goldberg, *The Power of Photography: How Photographs Changed Our Lives,* 229–37.

8. Barbie Zelizer, *Remembering to Forget: Holocaust Memory Through the Camera's Eye,* 56.

9. During the investigation, *U.S. News & World Report* questioned the credibility of several veterans who had provided the AP with testimonies. The media paid especially close attention to a doubt raised concerning a veteran, Edward Daily, whose provocative remarks had been repeatedly quoted in numerous news articles. It was revealed that Daily had not even been at the site of the incident. Since the Daily scandal, although the Pulitzer board officially reaffirmed the credibility of the AP's account, a backlash against the veracity of oral memories has taken place at newspapers across America.

10. Secretary of Defense William Cohen's entire statement can be found at http://www.pbs.org/newshour/media/media_watch/jan-june01/cohen_1-11.html.

11. William J. Clinton, statement on the incident at No Gun Ri (January 11, 2001), http://www.pbs.org/newshour/media/media_watch/jan-june01/clinton_1-11 .html.

12. Erving Goffman, *Relations in Public: Microstudies of the Public Order,* 119.

13. The list of narrators includes Chung Eun-Youg and Park Sun-Yong, who lost both their five-year-old son and their two-year-old daughter; Chung Koo-Ho, who lost her mother; Chung Koo-Hun and Chung Myong-Ja, whose mother and sister died; Chung Koo-Hak, a brother of Koo-Hun and Myong-Ja, whose face was disfigured; Yang Hae-Sook, who lost her left eye; Yang Hae-Chan, a brother of Hae-Sook; Chun Choon-Ja, who lost her mother, brother, and grandfather; Chun Ok-Boon, an aunt of Chun Choon-Ja; Keum Cho-Ja, whose right hip was disfigured; and Chung Koo-Do, a son of Chung Eun-Yong and Park Sun-Young, the latter a spokesperson for the Committee for Unveiling Truth about the No Gun Ri Massacre.

14. Barbara Allen, "Re-creating the Past: The Narrator's Perspective in Oral History."

15. Maurice Halbwachs, *The Collective Memory;* David Lowenthal, *The Past Is a Foreign Country;* John Bodnar, *Remaking America: Public Memory, Commemoration, and Patriotism in the Twentieth Century;* Zelizer, *Remembering to Forget;* Michael Schudson, *Watergate in American Memory: How We Remember, Forget, and Reconstruct the Past;* Barry Schwartz, *Abraham Lincoln and the Forge of National Memory;* Carolyn Kitch, *History and Memory in American Magazines.*

16. Antonio Gramsci, *Selections from the Prison Notebooks.*

17. Halbwachs, *The Collective Memory,* 70.

18. Michael Kammen, *Mystic Chords of Memory: The Transformation of Tradition in American Culture;* Barbara A. Biesecker, "Remembering World War II: The Rhetoric and Politics of National Commemoration at the Turn of the 21st Century."

19. John Bodnar, "Power and Memory in Oral History: Workers and Managers at Studebaker," 1202.

20. Marita Sturken, *Tangled Memories: The Vietnam War, the AIDS Epidemic, and the Politics of Remembering*, 2.

21. John R. Gillis, "Memory and Identity: The History of a Relationship," 7; Claudia Koonz, "Between Memory and Oblivion: Concentration Camps in German Memory," 258; Yosefa Loshitzky, "Inverting Images of the '40s: The Berlin Wall and Collective Amnesia."

22. Diane F. Britton, "Public History and Public Memory"; Biesecker, "Remembering World War II"; Jenny Edkins, "The Rush to Memory and the Rhetoric of War."

23. John Osborne, "The Ugly War"; Carl Mydans, *More than Meets the Eye*, 291–93; Max Hastings, *The Korean War*, 42–45; Phillip Knightley, *The First Casualty: The War Correspondent as Hero and Myth-Maker from the Crimea to Iraq*, 374.

24. Mangil Kang, *Hanguk hyoundaesa* [Korean contemporary history]; Janggip Choi, "One Understanding Regarding the Korean War"; Carter J. Eckert et al., *Korea Old and New: A History*, 305–26; Bruce Cumings, *Korea's Place in the Sun: A Modern History*, 139–84.

25. Bruce Cumings, "American Policy and Korean Liberation"; John Merrill, "Internal Warfare in Korea, 1948–1950: The Local Setting of the Korean War"; Eckert et al., *Korea Old and New*, 337–39.

26. Eckert et al., *Korea Old and New*, 338.

27. Paul G. Pierpaoli Jr., "Beyond Collective Amnesia: A Korean War Retrospective," 93.

28. Bruce Cumings and William Stueck, cited in "Pentagon Says It Can Find No Proof of Massacre," *New York Times*, September 30, 1999.

29. Pentagon briefing by Louis Caldera, secretary of the U.S. Army, cited in "U.S. to Revisit Accusations of a Massacre by G.I.'s in '50," *New York Times*, October 1, 1999.

30. Marguerite Higgins, *War in Korea: The Report of a Woman Combat Correspondent*, 86.

31. "Text of Truman's 'Report to Nation' on Korea War," *New York Times*, September 2, 1950.

32. "Casualities of an Unready Army," *Boston Globe*, October 2, 1999.

33. "Clinton Honors Those Who Died, Praises Spending Bill for Military," *St. Petersburg (FL) Times*, November 12, 1999.

34. Sang-Hun Choe, Charles J. Hanley, and Martha Mendoza, "The Bridge at No Gun Ri."

35. Cited in Choe, Hanley, and Mendoza, "War's Hidden Chapter."

36. Cornelius Osgood, *The Koreans and Their Culture*, 35.

37. Sahr Conway-Lanz, "Beyond No Gun Ri: Refugees and the United States Military in the Korean War."

38. Yangban was the dominant social class of the Choson Dynasty. People in the Yangban class were studying and cultivating an ideal of Confucian doctrines and served society as civil or military officials. They had little interest in working at any technical posts, agriculture, manufacture, or trading business. Eckert et al., *Korea Old and New*, 108–9.

39. These headlines appeared in the *New York Times*, September 30, 1999; *Washington Post*, September 30, 1999; and *Chicago Tribune*, September 30, 1999.

40. Chun Choon-Ja. She was eleven years old and lost her mother, brother, and grandfather in the incident.

41. Chung Koo Ho. He was thirteen years old and lost his mother in the incident.

42. Osborne, "The Ugly War," 21; Hastings, *The Korean War*, 82.

43. Osborne, "The Ugly War," 21.

44. *Cho Sun In Min Bo* was a tabloid newspaper founded in 1945. As one of the progressive newspapers, it had criticized most policies of the U.S. Army Military Government in Korea and had been assailed several times by youth groups of right-wing factions of the political force. In 1946, the U.S. Army Military Government had ordered *Cho Sun In Min Bo* to stop publication. See Minhwan Kim, *Hanguk Sinmunsa* [The history of Korean newspaper].

45. Linda Shopes, "Oral History and Community Involvement: The Baltimore Neighborhood Heritage Project"; Bodnar, "Power and Memory in Oral History"; Michael Kammen, "Public History and the Uses of Memory."

46. "The Fallout from No Gun Ri: Should the U.S. Apologize for Korean War Casualties?," *Plain Dealer*, November 21, 1999.

47. Cumings, *Korea's Place in the Sun*; Kang, *Hanguk hyoundaesa*.

48. Osgood, *Koreans and Their Culture*, 22–23.

49. Robert R. Archibald, "A Personal History of Memory," 66.

50. Edward Hallett Carr, *What Is History?*, 35.

2. "SCRIPTING" MEMORIES

1. Sidonie Smith and Julia Watson, *Reading Autobiography: A Guide for Interpreting Life Narratives*, 23.

2. Ibid., 27.

3. James E. Young, "Between History and Memory: The Voice of the Eyewitness," 277.

4. Lynn Hanley, *Writing War: Fiction, Gender, and Memory*, 7.

5. Zelizer, *Remembering to Forget*.

6. Cathy Caruth, *Unclaimed Experience: Trauma, Narrative, and History*; Smith and Watson, *Reading Autobiography*; Edkins, "Rush to Memory."

7. Caruth, *Unclaimed Experience*, 58.

8. Smith and Watson, *Reading Autobiography,* 22.

9. Edkins, "Rush to Memory," 39.

10. Chungmoo Choi, "Korean Women in a Culture of Inequality," 107.

11. Elizabeth Choi, "Statues of the Family and Motherhood for Korean Women."

12. John Duncan, "Confucian Social Values in Contemporary South Korea."

13. C. Choi, "Korean Women in a Culture of Inequality"; Duncan, "Confucian Social Values in Contemporary South Korea."

14. Seungsook Moon, *Militarized Modernity and Gendered Citizenship in South Korea.*

15. Martina Deuchler, "Propagating Female Virtues in Choson Korea," 143.

16. E. Choi, "Statues of the Family," 191–92.

17. Karlyn Kohrs Campbell, "The Sound of Women's Voices."

18. C. Choi, "Korean Women in a Culture of Inequality," 104.

19. Suzette A. Henke, *Trauma and Testimony in Women's Life-Writing,* xii.

20. Smith and Watson, *Reading Autobiography,* 22.

21. Chung, *Gdai, Wooriyi Apumyul Anunga?*

22. Bodnar, "Power and Memory in Oral History"; Paul Thompson, *The Voice of the Past: Oral History.*

23. Young, "Between History and Memory," 281.

24. Kathryn Anderson and Dana C. Jack, "Learning to Listen: Interview Techniques and Analyses."

25. Bernard Trainor, "The Anguish of Knowing: What Happened at No Gun Ri," *Washington Post,* January 21, 2001.

26. Roland Barthes, "Rhetoric of the Image."

27. Lowenthal, *Past Is a Foreign Country,* 218.

28. L. Hanley, *Writing War,* 134.

29. Caruth, *Unclaimed Experience,* 4.

3. "SANITIZING" MEMORIES

1. Karal A. Marling and John Wetenhall, "The Sexual Politics of Memory: The Vietnam Women's Memorial Project and 'the Wall.'"

2. Pierpaoli, "Beyond Collective Amnesia," 92.

3. Carole Blair, Marsha S. Jeppeson, and Enrico Pucci Jr., "Public Memorializing in Postmodernity: The Vietnam Veterans Memorial as Prototype"; Charles L. Griswold, "The Vietnam Veterans Memorial and the Washington Mall: Philosophical Thoughts on Political Iconography"; Harry W. Haines, "'What Kind of War?': An Analysis of the Vietnam Veterans Memorial"; Sturken, *Tangled Memories.*

4. Robert J. Lentz, *Korean War Filmography.*

5. Paul Fussell, *The Great War and Modern Memory;* Jay Winter, *Remembering War: The Great War Between Memory and History in the Twentieth Century.*

6. James E. Young, *The Texture of Memory: Holocaust Memorials and Meaning;* Zelizer, *Remembering to Forget.*

7. Biesecker, "Remembering World War II."

8. Sturken, *Tangled Memories;* Robert Hariman and John L. Lucaites, "Public Identity and Collective Memory in U.S. Iconic Photography: The Image of 'Accidental Napalm.'"

9. Douglas Kellner, "Reading the Gulf War: Production/Text/Reception"; Andrew Hoskins, *Televising War: From Vietnam to Iraq.*

10. Howard Schuman and Jacqueline Scott, "Generations and Collective Memories," 362.

11. Kathryn Weathersby, "The Soviet Role in the Early Phase of the Korean War: New Documentary Evidence."

12. Pierpaoli, "Beyond Collective Amnesia."

13. Michael Dobbs, "War and Remembrance: Truth and Other Casualties of No Gun Ri," *Washington Post,* May 21, 2000.

14. Jack Saunders, "Records in the National Archives Relating to Korea, 1945–1950."

15. Merrill, "Internal Warfare in Korea"; Kang, *Hanguk hyoundaesa;* Jang-gip Choi, *Hanguk joenjang youngu: Hanguk hyundaesayi ihae* [Studying the Korean War: Understanding Korean contemporary history]; Eckert et al., *Korea Old and New;* Cumings, *Korea's Place in the Sun;* Pierpaoli, "Beyond Collective Amnesia."

16. Bruce Cumings, *War and Television,* 7.

17. Ibid., 130.

18. Pierpaoli, "Beyond Collective Amnesia," 92.

19. Barthes, "Rhetoric of the Image."

20. Barry Schwartz, "Frame Images: Towards a Semiotics of Collective Memory"; Barbie Zelizer, "Collective Memories, Images, and the Atrocity of War," in *Remembering to Forget,* by Zelizer, 1–15.

21. Paul Messaris, *Visual Literacy: Image, Mind, and Reality;* Sandra E. Moriarty, "The Symbiotics of Semiotics and Visual Communication."

22. Stuart Hall, "The Spectacle of the 'Other'"; Zelizer, "Collective Memories, Images, and the Atrocity of War"; Fred Ritchin, *In Our Own Image: The Coming Revolution in Photography;* Marita Sturken and Lisa Cartwright, *Practices of Looking: An Introduction to Visual Culture.*

23. Zelizer, "Collective Memories, Images, and the Atrocity of War."

24. Bill Nichols, "The Voice of Documentary"; Bill Nichols, *Representing Reality: Issues and Concepts in Documentary;* Claudia Springer, "Vietnam: A

Television History and the Equivocal Nature of Objectivity"; Trinh T. Minh-ha, "Documentary Is/Not a Name"; Jay Ruby, *Picturing Culture: Explorations of Film and Anthropology.*

25. Nichols, *Representing Reality.*

26. Barthes, "Rhetoric of the Image."

27. Jeanne Allen, "Self-Reflexivity in Documentary"; Joanna C. Scherer, "You Can't Believe Your Eyes: Inaccuracies in Photographs of North American Indians"; Sturken and Cartwright, *Practices of Looking.*

28. Scherer, "You Can't Believe Your Eyes," 67.

29. Robert Hamilton, "Image and Context: The Production and Reproduction of the Execution of a VC Suspect by Eddie Adams"; Victor Caldaroal, "Time and Television War"; Kellner, "Reading the Gulf War."

30. Cumings, *Korea's Place in the Sun.*

31. Eckert et al., *Korea Old and New.*

32. Hoskins, *Televising War.*

33. Wilfred G. Burchett, *Again Korea.*

34. Conway-Lanz, "Beyond No Gun Ri."

35. Mitchel P. Roth, *Historical Dictionary of War Journalism;* Miles Hudson and John Stanier, *War and the Media: A Random Searchlight;* Greg McLaughlin, *The War Correspondent.*

36. Hudson and Stanier, *War and the Media.*

37. Nicholas Garnham, "TV Documentary and Ideology"; J. Allen, "Self-Reflexivity in Documentary"; Ruby, *Picturing Culture.*

38. J. Allen, "Self-Reflexivity in Documentary."

39. Nichols, *Introduction to Documentary.*

40. Nichols, "The Voice of Documentary."

41. Robert Brent Toplin, "The Filmmaker as Historian," 1216.

42. Springer, "Vietnam."

43. Eckert et al., *Korea Old and New.*

44. Sturken, *Tangled Memories,* 4.

45. "About PBS," http://www.pbs.org/insidepbs.

46. Merrill, "Internal Warfare in Korea"; Kang, *Hanguk hyoundaesa;* J. Choi, *Hanguk joenjang youngu;* Eckert et al., *Korea Old and New;* Cumings, *Korea's Place in the Sun.*

47. Kang, *Hanguk hyoundaesa.*

48. Cumings, "American Policy and Korean Liberation," 49.

49. Eckert et al., *Korea Old and New.*

50. Cumings, *Korea's Place in the Sun,* 245.

51. Eckert et al., *Korea Old and New,* 335.

52. Bodnar, *Remaking America.*

1. I interviewed three veterans who participated in building the memorial: Don G. Reaveley (the chair of the Utah Korean War Memorial Committee), A. J. Staker (a committee member), and Frederick E. Peyton (a committee member). I also interviewed Val Pope (the director of the Park Division in Salt Lake City) and Mark Duvenport (a designer of the memorial). In order to gain insight on local veterans' memories of the war, I interviewed two additional Utahn Korean War veterans, John A. Young and Carl L. R. McBirnie.

2. The U.S. Department of Defense Commemoration of the 50th Anniversary of the Korean War, http://korea50.army.mil/welcome.shtml.

3. David Glassberg, "Remembering a War"; Patrick Hagopian, "The Kentucky Vietnam Veterans Memorial."

4. David Halberstam, *The Coldest Winter: America and the Korean War,* 2.

5. Halbwachs, *The Collective Memory,* 48.

6. Ibid., 50–51.

7. Louis Althusser, "Ideology and Ideological State Apparatus," in *Lenin and Philosophy, and Other Essays.*

8. Halbwachs, *The Collective Memory*; Pierre Nora, "Between Memory and History: Les lieux de memoire"; Barbie Zelizer, "Reading the Past Against the Grain: The Shape of Memory Studies"; Sturken, *Tangled Memories*; Winter, *Remembering War.*

9. Michael Adams, *The Best War Ever: America and World War II*; Nina Tumarkin, *The Living and the Dead: The Rise and Fall of the Cult of World War II in Russia*; Biesecker, "Remembering World War II"; Catherine Merridale, *Ivan's War: Life and Death in the Red Army, 1939–1945*; John Bodnar, *The "Good War" in American Memory.*

10. Edward T. Linenthal, "Anatomy of a Controversy"; Theodore O. Proisis, "The Collective Memory of the Atomic Bombings Misrecognized as Objective History: The Case of the Public Opposition to the National Air and Space Museum's Atom Bomb Exhibit"; Lisa Yoneyama, "For Transformative Knowledge and Postnationalist Public Sphere: The Smithsonian *Enola Gay* Controversy."

11. Bodnar, *"Good War" in American Memory,* 91.

12. Biesecker, "Remembering World War II."

13. Merridale, *Ivan's War.*

14. George L. Mosse, *Fallen Soldiers: Reshaping the Memory of the World Wars.*

15. Winter, *Remembering War,* 140.

16. Lowenthal, *Past Is a Foreign Country*; Maurice Halbwachs, *On Collective Memory.*

17. Barry Schwartz, "The Social Context of Commemoration: A Study in Collective Memory"; Michael Schudson, "The Present in the Past Versus the Past in the Present."

18. "The Home Front Becomes Aware of Korea," 47.

19. David Halberstam, *The Fifties*, 70.

20. Douglas T. Miller and Marion Nowak, *The Fifties: The Way We Really Were*, 23.

21. Pierpaoli, "Beyond Collective Amnesia."

22. "War Brought Home to Us," *Salt Lake Tribune*, November 20, 1951.

23. Amartya Sen, *Identity and Violence: The Illusion of Destiny*.

24. "U.S. Military Personnel Who Died from Hostile Action (Including Missing and Captured) in the Korean War, 1950–1957," http://www.archives.gov/research/korean-war/casualty-lists/ut-alpha.html.

25. Benjamin Urrutia, "The Korean War and Utah"; Richard C. Roberts, "The Utah National Guard and Territorial Militias."

26. Pierpaoli, "Beyond Collective Amnesia."

27. James L. Clayton, "The Impact of the Cold War on the Economies of California and Utah, 1946–1965."

28. Ibid.; Thomas G. Alexander and Rick J. Fish, "The Defense Industry of Utah."

29. William G. Love, "A History of Memory Grove."

30. Terry T. Williams, *Refugee: An Unnatural History of Family and Place*.

31. "Beloved Grove Now Just a Memory," *Salt Lake Tribune*, August 13, 1999.

32. Appropriation for Memory Grove Tornado Recovery Efforts, http://www.le.state.ut.us/~2001/bills/hbillint/HB0097.htm.

33. Val Pope, interview by the author, September 10, 2008.

34. Don B. Reaveley, interview by the author, February 16, 2007.

35. A. J. Stoker, interview by the author, November 12, 2008.

36. Linda Granfield, *I Remember Korea: Veterans Tell Their Stories of the Korean War, 1950–53*; Richard Peters and Xiaobing Li, *Voices from the Korean War: Personal Stories of American, Korean, and Chinese Soldiers*.

37. Bruce Cumings, "How and Why We Remember the Korean War," panel discussion of the Korea Society at Seoul, South Korea, January 16, 2008, http://www.koreasociety.org/external/podcast.html.

38. For designing the contents of the wall, the committee then selected local designer Mark Duvenport, whose name became known to the community after he completed a war monument at American Fork City Cemetery in 1991. However, Duvenport's initial idea of incorporating a bronze collage and a statue into the memorial turned out to be too expensive for the limited budget. Thus, using Duvenport's basic drawing, veterans themselves became a task force for inventing an integral yet affordable design for the memorial.

39. Don Reaveley, remarks at the dedication ceremony, July 27, 2003.

40. Such a collage did not take shape in a vacuum. The land that the city granted the veterans' committee for the memorial was a lot that formerly

displayed armored personnel carriers. Thus, the platform of the carriers became the template within which veterans had to design the memorial. To incorporate the remnant of the concrete platform into a new memorial, veterans decided to pick up the V shape of the wall as a basic canvas.

41. Mosse, *Fallen Soldiers.*

42. Sturken, *Tangled Memories.*

43. Philippe Ariès, "Thy Death."

44. Merrill, "Internal Warfare in Korea"; Miles Hudson and John Stanier, "The Asian Connection: Korea and Vietnam," in *War and the Media,* by Hudson and Stanier, 85–120; Bruce Cumings, "Occurrence at Nogun-Ri Bridge: An Inquiry into the History and Memory of a Civil War."

45. Winter, *Remembering War,* 44.

46. Barney Oldfield, "USAF Press Relations in the Far East."

47. Sturken, *Tangled Memories;* Carole Blair and Neil Michel, "The AIDS Memorial Quilt and the Contemporary Culture of Public Commemoration."

48. Sturken, *Tangled Memories.*

49. Pierpaoli, "Beyond Collective Amnesia."

50. Adams, *Best War Ever.*

51. James M. Mayo, *War Memorials as Political Landscape: The American Experience and Beyond.*

52. Daniel L. Schacter, *The Seven Sins of Memory: How the Mind Forgets and Remembers,* 5.

53. Joe Bauman, "Utahn Reliving Memories of Bitter N. Korea Battle," *Deseret News,* May 31, 2004.

54. A. J. Stoker, interview by the author, November 12, 2008.

55. Frederick Peyton, interview by the author, October 29, 2008.

56. Carl L. R. McBirnie, interview by the author, November 12, 2008.

57. Don B. Reaveley, interview by the author, February 16, 2007.

58. Data on veterans of the Korean War, U.S. Department of Veterans Affairs, http://www1.va.gov/vetdata/docs/KW2000.doc.

59. Lewis H. Carlson, *Remembered Prisoners of a Forgotten War: An Oral History of Korean War POWs.*

60. Excerpted from a letter by Kim Dae-Jung, June 25, 2000.

61. Bodnar, *"Good War" in American Memory,* 85.

62. Ferdinand de Saussure, "Nature of the Linguistic Sign and Immutability and Mutability of the Sign."

5. "SHATTERING" MEMORIES

1. See the following references: "Upheaval in the East: Lenin Statue in Mothballs," *New York Times,* December 11, 1989; "Albania Removes Statues of Stalin,"

New York Times, December 22, 1990; "Goff's Lenin Statue"; *Russian Life,* letter to the editors, March–April 2004; "Boom Town Breaks Free of Its Bonds," USA *Today,* June 11, 2004.

2. Mikhail Yampolsky, "In the Shadow of Monuments: Notes on Iconoclasm and Time"; Theresa Sabonis-Chafee, "Communism as Kitsch: Soviet Symbols in Post-Soviet Society"; Katherine Verdery, *The Political Lives of Dead Bodies: Reburial and Postsocialist Change;* Monica Popescu, "Translations: Lenin's Statues, Post-communism, and Post-apartheid"; Beverly A. James, *Imagining Postcommunism: Visual Narratives of Hungary's 1956 Revolution;* Sergei Kruk, "Semiotics of Visual Iconicity in Leninist 'Monumental' Propaganda."

3. Tumarkin, *Living and Dead;* Brian Ladd, *The Ghosts of Berlin: Confronting German History in the Urban Landscape;* Sergiusz Michalski, *Public Monuments: Art in Political Bondage, 1870–1997;* Sanford Levinson, *Written in Stone: Public Monuments in Changing Societies;* Karen E. Till, *The New Berlin: Memory, Politics, Place;* Jeffrey K. Olick, "What Does It Mean to Normalize the Past? Official Memory in German Politics Since 1989"; Jeffrey K. Olick, *In the House of the Hangman: The Agonies of German Defeat, 1943–1949;* Jeffrey K. Olick, *The Politics of Regret: On Collective Memory and Historical Responsibility;* Paul Stangl, "Revolutionaries' Cemeteries in Berlin: Memory, History, Place, and Space."

4. Tumarkin, *Living and Dead.*

5. Barthes, "Rhetoric of the Image."

6. Kirk Savage, *Standing Soldiers, Kneeling Slaves: Race, War, and Monument in Nineteenth-Century America,* 8.

7. Halbwachs, *The Collective Memory.*

8. Tumarkin, *Living and Dead;* Ladd, *Ghosts of Berlin;* Victor Roudometof, *Collective Memory, National Identity, and Ethnic Conflict: Greece, Bulgaria, and the Macedonian Question;* Till, *New Berlin;* Olick, "What Does It Mean to Normalize the Past?"; Olick, *In the House of the Hangman;* Olick, *The Politics of Regret;* Stangl, "Revolutionaries' Cemeteries in Berlin"; Roger C. Aden, "Redefining the 'Cradle of Liberty': The President's House Controversy in Independence National Historical Park."

9. Verdery, *Political Lives of Dead Bodies,* 5.

10. Nina Tumarkin, *Lenin Lives! The Lenin Cult in Soviet Russia.*

11. Young, *Texture of Memory,* 14.

12. Mosse, *Fallen Soldiers;* Aden, "Redefining the 'Cradle of Liberty.'"

13. Michael North, "The Public as Sculpture: From Heavenly City to Mass Ornament."

14. James E. Young, "The Counter-monument: Memory Against Itself in Germany Today"; Michalski, *Public Monuments.*

15. Saussure, "Nature of the Linguistic Sign," 74.

16. Young, "Counter-monument"; Young, *Texture of Memory;* Carole Blair, "Contemporary U.S. Memorial Sites as Exemplars of Rhetoric's Materiality"; Verdery, *Political Lives of Dead Bodies;* Greg Dickinson, Carole Blair, and Brian L. Ott, *Places of Public Memory: The Rhetoric of Museums and Memorials.*

17. Young, *Texture of Memory.*

18. Halbwachs, *The Collective Memory.*

19. Robert R. Archibald, "A Personal History of Memory."

20. Andreas W. Daum, "Capitals in Modern History: Inventing Urban Spaces for the Nation"; Stangl, "Revolutionaries' Cemeteries in Berlin"; Janet Jacobs, "Memorializing the Sacred: Kristallnacht in German National Memory"; Aden, "Redefining the 'Cradle of Liberty'"; Dickinson, Blair, and Ott, *Places of Public Memory.*

21. Maoz Azaryahu, "The Politics of Commemorative Street Renaming: Berlin, 1945–1948."

22. Levinson, *Written in Stone.*

23. Mayo, *War Memorials as Political Landscape,* 1.

24. Blair, "Contemporary U.S. Memorial Sites"; Dickinson, Blair, and Ott, *Places of Public Memory.*

25. Geoffrey Hartman, *Bitburg in Moral and Political Perspective;* Olick, "What Does It Mean to Normalize the Past?"; Olick, *In the House of the Hangman;* Olick, *The Politics of Regret.*

26. Marita Sturken, "The Wall and the Screen Memory," in *Tangled Memories,* by Sturken, 44–84; Blair, "Contemporary U.S. Memorial Sites."

27. North, "Public as Sculpture," 861.

28. James Carey, *Communication as Culture: Essays on Media and Society.*

29. Daniel Dayan and Elihu Katz, *Media Events: The Live Broadcasting of History.*

30. Kevin DeLuca and Jennifer Peeples, "From Public Sphere to Public Screen: Democracy, Activism, and the 'Violence' of Seattle."

31. It may not be coincidental that the statue of MacArthur was erected in 1957, a controversial year during which the United States, in seeking an introduction of advanced weapons into South Korea, unilaterally broke an armistice agreement that was intended to prevent both sides from being further militarized with new types of weapons. See Cumings, *Korea's Place in the Sun,* 478.

32. Jung-Gu Office Incheon City, *Tourism Information Guide for Jung-Gu Incheon,* 49.

33. Michael Schaller, *Douglas MacArthur: The Far Eastern General,* 183.

34. Eun-Jung Cho, "The Study on the Relations Between the First Republic of Korea and the Art."

35. Yampolsky, "In the Shadow of Monuments."

36. Schaller, *Douglas MacArthur;* Ronald H. Carpenter, "General Douglas MacArthur's Oratory on Behalf of Inchon: Discourse That Altered the Course of History."

37. Bruce Cumings, *The Korean War.*

38. Mayo, *War Memorials as Political Landscape,* 40.

39. Michalski, *Public Monuments.*

40. Beverly A. James, "Envisioning Postcommunism: Budapest's Stalin Monument," 166.

41. Cho, "Study on the Relations."

42. Sun-Joo Kim, "The Current Debate and Implication Regarding the Destruction of the Statue of MacArthur"; Chang-Jun Jang, "Is General MacArthur Really a Hero of the Republic of Korea?"

43. Tom Pauken, "Claiming MacArthur a War Maniac," *Korean Time,* October 25, 2005.

44. C. Hanley and Mendoza, "Bridge at No Gun Ri"; Conway-Lanz, "Beyond No Gun Ri."

45. Burchett, *Again Korea;* Schaller, *Douglas MacArthur;* Cumings, *Korea's Place in the Sun;* Conway-Lanz, "Beyond No Gun Ri."

46. Bruce Cumings, "War Is a Stern Teacher."

47. James, "Envisioning Postcommunism," 159.

48. Verdery, *Political Lives of Dead Bodies,* 5.

49. Yampolsky, "In the Shadow of Monuments," 100.

50. "MacArthur Statue, the Transformation into a Yellowish Bronze," *Hanguk Il-bo,* December 6, 2005, 9.

51. Kevin DeLuca, *Image Politics: The New Rhetoric of Environmental Activism,* 1–22.

52. DeLuca and Peeples, "From Public Sphere to Public Screen."

53. Yampolsky, "In the Shadow of Monuments," 100.

54. Benedict Anderson, *Imagined Communities: Reflections on the Origin and Spread of Nationalism;* Roudometof, *Collective Memory, National Identity, and Ethnic Conflict;* Michael E. Geisler, "Introduction: What Are National Symbols— and What Do They Do to Us?"

EPILOGUE

1. "North Korea's Fear of B-52 . . . Nightmare of B-29 During the Korean War . . . ," *Choongang Il-bo,* http://article.joinsmsn.com/news/article/article.asp?total_id=11018279&cloc=olink|article|default.

Adams, Michael. *The Best War Ever: America and World War II.* Baltimore: Johns Hopkins University Press, 1994.

Aden, Roger C. "Redefining the 'Cradle of Liberty': The President's House Controversy in Independence National Historical Park." *Rhetoric and Public Affairs* 13, no. 2 (2010): 251–80.

Alexander, Thomas G., and Rick J. Fish. "The Defense Industry of Utah." In *Utah Historical Encyclopedia,* 129–32. Salt Lake City: University of Utah Press.

Allen, Barbara. "Re-creating the Past: The Narrator's Perspective in Oral History." *Oral History Review* 12 (1984): 1–12.

Allen, Jeanne. "Self-Reflexivity in Documentary." *Cine-tracts* 1, no. 2 (1977): 37–43.

Althusser, Louis. "Ideology and Ideological State Apparatus." In *Lenin and Philosophy, and Other Essays,* 85–126. 1971. Reprint, New York: Monthly Review Press, 2001.

Anderson, Benedict. *Imagined Communities: Reflections on the Origin and Spread of Nationalism.* London: Verso, 1991.

Anderson, Kathryn, and Dana C. Jack. "Learning to Listen: Interview Techniques and Analyses." In *The Oral History Reader,* edited by R. Perks and A. Thomson, 157–71. New York: Routledge, 1998.

Archibald, Robert R. "A Personal History of Memory." In *Social Memory and History: Anthropological Perspectives,* edited by J. J. Climo and M. G. Cattell, 65–80. Walnut Creek: Aha Mija Press, 2002.

Ariès, Philippe. "Thy Death." In *Western Attitudes toward Death from the Middle Ages to the Present,* translated by Patricia Ranum, 55–82. Baltimore: Johns Hopkins University Press, 1974.

Azaryahu, Maoz. "The Politics of Commemorative Street Renaming: Berlin, 1945–1948." *Journal of Historical Geography* 37, no. 4 (2011): 483–92.

Barthes, Roland. "Rhetoric of the Image." In *Image-Music-Text,* translated by S. Heath, 32–51. 1964. Reprint, New York: Hill and Wang, 1977.

Biesecker, Barbara A. "Remembering World War II: The Rhetoric and Politics of National Commemoration at the Turn of the 21st Century." *Quarterly Journal of Speech* 88, no. 4 (2002): 393–409.

Blair, Carole. "Contemporary U.S. Memorial Sites as Exemplars of Rhetoric's Materiality." In *Rhetorical Bodies,* edited by J. Selzer and S. Crowley, 16–57. Madison: University of Wisconsin Press, 1999.

Blair, Carole, Marsha S. Jeppeson, and Enrico Pucci Jr. "Public Memorializing in Postmodernity: The Vietnam Veterans Memorial as Prototype." *Quarterly Journal of Speech* 77 (1991): 263–388.

Blair, Carole, and Neil Michel. "The AIDS Memorial Quilt and the Contemporary Culture of Public Commemoration." *Rhetoric and Public Affairs* 10, no. 4 (2007): 595–626.

Bodnar, John. *The "Good War" in American Memory*. Baltimore: Johns Hopkins University Press, 2010.

——. "Power and Memory in Oral History: Workers and Managers at Studebaker." *Journal of American History* 75, no. 4 (1989): 1201–21.

——. *Remaking America: Public Memory, Commemoration, and Patriotism in the Twentieth Century*. Princeton, NJ: Princeton University Press, 1992.

Britton, Diane F. "Public History and Public Memory." *Public Historian* 19, no. 3 (1997): 1–17.

Burchett, Wilfred G. *Again Korea*. New York: International Publishers, 1968.

Caldaroal, Victor. "Time and Television War." *Public Culture* 4, no. 2 (1992): 127–36.

Campbell, Karlyn Kohrs. "The Sound of Women's Voices." *Quarterly Journal of Speech* 75 (1989): 212–58.

Carey, James. *Communication as Culture: Essays on Media and Society*. New York: Routledge, 1989.

Carlson, Lewis H. *Remembered Prisoners of a Forgotten War: An Oral History of Korean War POWs*. New York: St. Martin's / Griffin, 2002.

Carpenter, Ronald H. "General Douglas MacArthur's Oratory on Behalf of Inchon: Discourse That Altered the Course of History." *Southern Communication Journal* 58, no. 1 (1992): 1–12.

Carr, Edward Hallett. *What Is History?* New York: Vintage Books, 1961.

Caruth, Cathy. *Unclaimed Experience: Trauma, Narrative, and History*. Baltimore: Johns Hopkins University Press, 1991.

Cho, Eun-Jung. "The Study on the Relations Between the First Republic of Korea and the Art." Ph.D. diss., Ehwa University, South Korea, 2005.

Choe, Sang-Hun, Charles J. Hanley, and Martha Mendoza. "The Bridge at No Gun Ri." *Dissent* 47 (2000): 39–43.

Choi, Chungmoo. "Korean Women in a Culture of Inequality." In *Korea Briefing*, edited by D. N. Clark, 97–116. Boulder, CO: Westview, 1992.

Choi, Elizabeth. "Statues of the Family and Motherhood for Korean Women." In *Women of Japan and Korea: Continuity and Change*, edited by J. Gelb and M. L. Palley, 189–205. Philadelphia: Temple University Press, 1994.

Choi, Janggip. *Hanguk joenjang youngu: Hanguk hyundaesayi ihae* [Studying the Korean War: Understanding Korean contemporary history]. Vol. 1. Seoul: Tae Am, 1990.

————. "One Understanding Regarding the Korean War." In *Hanguk Joenjang Youngu: Hanguk Hyundaesayi Ihae* [Studying Korean War: Understanding Korean contemporary history], 1:313–54. Seoul: Tae Am, 1990.

Chung, Eun-Yong. *Gdai, Wooriyi Apumyul Anunga?* [Do you know our pain?]. Seoul: Dari Media, 1994.

Clayton, James L. "The Impact of the Cold War on the Economies of California and Utah, 1946–1965." *Pacific Historical Review* 36 (1967): 449–73.

Conway-Lanz, Sahr. "Beyond No Gun Ri: Refugees and the United States Military in the Korean War." *Diplomatic History* 29, no. 1 (2005): 49–81.

Cumings, Bruce. "American Policy and Korean Liberation." In *Without Parallel: The American-Korean Relationship Since 1945,* edited by F. Baldwin, 39–108. New York: Pantheon, 1974.

————. *The Korean War.* New York: Modern Library, 2010.

————. *Korea's Place in the Sun: A Modern History.* New York: W. W. Norton, 1997.

————. "Occurrence at Nogun-Ri Bridge: An Inquiry into the History and Memory of a Civil War." *Critical Asian Studies* 33, no. 4 (2001): 509–26.

————. *War and Television.* New York: Verso, 1992.

————. "War Is a Stern Teacher." In *Living Through the Forgotten War: Portrait of Korea,* edited by P. Dowdey, 9–14. Middletown, CT: Mansfield Freeman Center, 2003.

Daum, Andreas W. "Capitals in Modern History: Inventing Urban Spaces for the Nation." In *Berlin-Washington, 1800–2000: Capital Cities, Cultural Representation, and National Identities,* edited by A. W. Daum and C. Mauch, 1–28. Cambridge: Cambridge University Press, 2005.

Dayan, Daniel, and Elihu Katz. *Media Events: The Live Broadcasting of History.* Cambridge, MA: Harvard University Press, 1992.

DeLuca, Kevin. *Image Politics: The New Rhetoric of Environmental Activism.* New York: Routledge, 1999.

DeLuca, Kevin, and Jennifer Peeples. "From Public Sphere to Public Screen: Democracy, Activism, and the 'Violence' of Seattle." *Critical Studies in Media Communication* 19, no. 2 (2002): 125–51.

Deuchler, Martina. "Propagating Female Virtues in Choson Korea." In *Women and Confucian Cultures in Premodern China, Korea, and Japan,* edited by D. Ko, J. K. Haboush, and J. A. Piggott, 142–69. Berkeley: University of California Press, 2003.

Dickinson, Greg, Carole Blair, and Brian L. Ott. *Places of Public Memory: The Rhetoric of Museums and Memorials.* Tuscaloosa: University of Alabama Press, 2010.

Duncan, John. "Confucian Social Values in Contemporary South Korea." In *Religion and Society in Contemporary Korea,* edited by L. R. Lancaster and R. K. Payne, 49–73. Berkeley: University of California Press, 1997.

Eckert, Carter J., Ki-Baik Lee, Young Ick Lew, Michael Robinson, and Edward W. Wagner. *Korea Old and New: A History.* Cambridge, MA: Harvard University Press, 1990.

Edkins, Jenny. "The Rush to Memory and the Rhetoric of War." *Journal of Political and Military Sociology* 31, no. 2 (2003): 231–50.

Fussell, Paul. *The Great War and Modern Memory.* New York: Oxford University Press, 1975.

Garnham, Nicholas. "TV Documentary and Ideology." *Screen* 13, no. 2 (1972): 109–15.

Geisler, Michael E. "Introduction: What Are National Symbols—and What Do They Do to Us?" In *National Symbols, Fractured Identities: Contesting the National Narrative,* edited by M. E. Geisler, 13–42. Middlebury, VT: Middlebury College Press, 2005.

Gillis, John R. "Memory and Identity: The History of a Relationship." Introduction to *Commemorations: The Politics of National Identity,* edited by J. R. Gillis, 3–24. Princeton, NJ: Princeton University Press, 1994.

Glassberg, David. "Remembering a War." In *Sense of History: The Place of the Past in American Life,* 25–57. Amherst: University of Massachusetts Press, 2001.

Goffman, Erving. *Relations in Public: Microstudies of the Public Order.* New York: Basic Books, 1971.

"Goff's Lenin Statue." *Texas Monthly* 21 (December 1993): 116.

Goldberg, Vicki. *The Power of Photography: How Photographs Changed Our Lives.* New York: Abbeville Publishing Group, 1993.

Gramsci, Antonio. *Selections from the Prison Notebooks.* Translated by Q. Hoare and G. N. Smith. New York: International Publishers, 1971.

Granfield, Linda. *I Remember Korea: Veterans Tell Their Stories of the Korean War, 1950–53.* New York: Clarion, 2003.

Griswold, Charles L. "The Vietnam Veterans Memorial and the Washington Mall: Philosophical Thoughts on Political Iconography." *Critical Inquiry* 12, no. 4 (1986): 688–719.

Hagopian, Patrick. "The Kentucky Vietnam Veterans Memorial." In *The Vietnam War in American Memory: Veterans, Memorials, and the Politics of Healing,* 231–67. Amherst: University of Massachusetts Press, 2009.

Haines, Harry W. "'What Kind of War?': An Analysis of the Vietnam Veterans Memorial." *Critical Studies in Mass Communication* 3, no. 1 (1986): 1–20.

Halberstam, David. *The Coldest Winter: America and the Korean War.* New York: Hyperion, 2007.

———. *The Fifties.* New York: Villard, 1993.

Halbwachs, Maurice. *The Collective Memory.* Translated by Francis J. Ditter Jr. and Vida Yazdi Ditter. 1950. Reprint, New York: Harper and Row, 1980.

———. *On Collective Memory.* Edited, translated, and with an introduction by Lewis A. Coser. Chicago: University of Chicago Press, 1992.

Hall, Stuart. "The Spectacle of the 'Other.'" In *Representation: Cultural Representations and Signifying Practices,* edited by Stuart Hall, 223–91. London: Sage, 1997.

Hamilton, Robert. "Image and Context: The Production and Reproduction of the Execution of a VC Suspect by Eddie Adams." In *Vietnam Images: War and Representation,* edited by J. Walsh and J. Aulich, 171–83. London: Macmillan, 1989.

Hanley, Charles J., Sang-Hun Choe, and Martha Mendoza. *The Bridge at No Gun Ri: A Hidden Nightmare from the Korean War.* New York: Henry Holt, 2001.

Hanley, Charles J., and Martha Mendoza. "The Bridge at No Gun Ri: Investigative Reporting, Hidden History, and Pulitzer Prize." *Harvard International Journal of Press Politics* 5, no. 4 (2000): 112–17.

Hanley, Lynn. *Writing War: Fiction, Gender, and Memory.* Amherst: University of Massachusetts Press, 1991.

Hariman, Robert, and John L. Lucaites. "Public Identity and Collective Memory in U.S. Iconic Photography: The Image of 'Accidental Napalm.'" *Critical Studies in Media Communication* 20, no. 1 (2003): 35–66.

Hartman, Geoffrey. *Bitburg in Moral and Political Perspective.* Bloomington: Indiana University Press, 1986.

Hastings, Max. *The Korean War.* New York: Simon and Schuster Paperbacks, 1987.

Henke, Suzette A. *Trauma and Testimony in Women's Life-Writing.* New York: St. Martin's, 2000.

Higgins, Marguerite. *War in Korea: The Report of a Woman Combat Correspondent.* New York: Doubleday, 1951.

"The Home Front Becomes Aware of Korea." *Life,* July 17, 1950.

Hoskins, Andrew. *Televising War: From Vietnam to Iraq.* London: Continuum, 2004.

Hudson, Miles, and John Stanier. *War and the Media: A Random Searchlight.* New York: New York University Press, 1998.

Jacobs, Janet. "Memorializing the Sacred: Kristallnacht in German National Memory." *Journal for the Scientific Study of Religion* 47, no. 3 (2008): 485–98.

James, Beverly A. "Envisioning Postcommunism: Budapest's Stalin Monument." In *Rhetorics of Display,* edited by L. J. Prell, 157–76. Columbia: University of South Carolina Press, 2006.

———. *Imagining Postcommunism: Visual Narratives of Hungary's 1956 Revolution.* College Station: Texas A&M University Press, 2005.

Jang, Chang-Jun. "Is General MacArthur Really a Hero of the Republic of Korea?" *Affairs and Movements* 107 (2005): 47–58.

Jung-Gu Office Incheon City. *Tourism Information Guide for Jung-Gu Incheon* (May 2008).

Kammen, Michael. *Mystic Chords of Memory: The Transformation of Tradition in American Culture* (New York: Vintage Books, 1993), 655–88.

———. "Public History and the Uses of Memory." *Public Historian* 19, no. 2 (1997): 49–52.

Kang, Mangil. *Hanguk hyoundaesa* [Korean contemporary history]. Seoul: Chang Jak and Bi Pyoung Sa, 1984.

Kellner, Douglas. "Reading the Gulf War: Production/Text/Reception." In *Media Culture: Cultural Studies, Identity, and Politics Between the Modern and the Postmodern,* 198–228. New York: Routledge, 1995.

Kim, Minhwan. *Hanguk Sinmunsa* [The history of Korean newspapers]. Seoul: Il Jo Gak, 1992.

Kim, Sun-Joo. "The Current Debate and Implication Regarding the Destruction of the Statue of MacArthur." *Affairs and Movements* 109 (2005): 15–21.

Kitch, Carolyn. *History and Memory in American Magazines.* Chapel Hill: University of North Carolina Press, 2005.

Knightley, Phillip. *The First Casualty: The War Correspondent as Hero and Myth-Maker from the Crimea to Iraq.* 3rd ed. Baltimore: Johns Hopkins University Press, 2004.

Koonz, Claudia. "Between Memory and Oblivion: Concentration Camps in German Memory." In *Commemorations: The Politics of National Identity,* edited by J. R. Gillis, 258–80. Princeton, NJ: Princeton University Press, 1994.

Kruk, Sergei. "Semiotics of Visual Iconicity in Leninist 'Monumental' Propaganda." *Visual Communication* 7, no. 1 (2008): 27–56.

Ladd, Brian. *The Ghosts of Berlin: Confronting German History in the Urban Landscape.* Chicago: University of Chicago Press, 1997.

Lentz, Robert J. *Korean War Filmography.* Jefferson, NC: McFarland, 2003.

Levinson, Sanford. *Written in Stone: Public Monuments in Changing Societies.* Durham, NC: Duke University Press, 1998.

Linenthal, Edward T. "Anatomy of a Controversy." In *History Wars: The* Enola Gay *and Other Battles for the American Past,* edited by E. T. Linenthal and T. Engelhardt, 9–62. New York: Metropolitan Books, 1996.

Loshitzky, Yosefa. "Inverting Images of the '40s: The Berlin Wall and Collective Amnesia." *Journal of Communication* 45, no. 2 (1995): 93–107.

Love, William G. "A History of Memory Grove." *Utah History Quarterly* 76, no. 2 (2008): 148–67.

Lowenthal, David. *The Past Is a Foreign Country.* New York: Cambridge University Press, 1985.

Marling, Karal A., and John Wetenhall. "The Sexual Politics of Memory: The Vietnam Women's Memorial Project and 'the Wall.'" *Prospects* 14 (1989): 341–72.

Mayo, James M. *War Memorials as Political Landscape: The American Experience and Beyond*. New York: Praeger, 1988.

McLaughlin, Greg. *The War Correspondent*. London: Pluto Press, 2002.

Merridale, Catherine. *Ivan's War: Life and Death in the Red Army, 1939–1945*. New York: Picador, 2006.

Merrill, John. "Internal Warfare in Korea, 1948–1950: The Local Setting of the Korean War." In *Child of Conflict: The Korean-American Relationship, 1943–1953*, edited by Bruce Cumings, 133–62. Seattle: University of Washington Press, 1983.

Messaris, Paul. *Visual Literacy: Image, Mind, and Reality*. Boulder, CO: Westview, 1994.

Michalski, Sergiusz. *Public Monuments: Art in Political Bondage, 1870–1997*. London: Reaktion Books, 1998.

Miller, Douglas T., and Marion Nowak. *The Fifties: The Way We Really Were*. New York: Doubleday, 1977.

Minh-ha, Trinh T. "Documentary Is/Not a Name." *October* 52 (1990): 77–100.

Moon, Seungsook. *Militarized Modernity and Gendered Citizenship in South Korea*. Durham, NC: Duke University Press, 2005.

Moriarty, Sandra E. "The Symbiotics of Semiotics and Visual Communication." *Journal of Visual Literacy* 22, no. 1 (2002): 19–28.

Mosse, George L. *Fallen Soldiers: Reshaping the Memory of the World Wars*. New York: Oxford University Press, 1990.

Mydans, Carl. *More than Meets the Eye*. New York: Harper and Brothers, 1959.

Nichols, Bill. *Introduction to Documentary*. Bloomington: Indiana University Press, 2001.

———. *Representing Reality: Issues and Concepts in Documentary*. Bloomington: Indiana University Press, 1991.

———. "The Voice of Documentary." *Film Quarterly* 35, no. 3 (1983): 20–30.

Nora, Pierre. "Between Memory and History: Les lieux de memoire." *Representations* 26 (1989): 7–25.

North, Michael. "The Public as Sculpture: From Heavenly City to Mass Ornament." *Critical Inquiry* 16, no. 4 (1990): 860–79.

Oldfield, Barney. "USAF Press Relations in the Far East." *Army Information Digest* (November 1950): 40–45.

Olick, Jeffrey K. *In the House of the Hangman: The Agonies of German Defeat, 1943–1949*. Chicago: University of Chicago Press, 2005.

———. *The Politics of Regret: On Collective Memory and Historical Responsibility*. New York: Routledge, 2007.

———. "What Does It Mean to Normalize the Past? Official Memory in German Politics Since 1989." In *States of Memory: Continuities, Conflicts, and*

Transformations in National Retrospection, 259–88. Durham, NC: Duke University Press, 2003.

Osborne, John. "The Ugly War." *Time* 56, no. 8 (1950): 20–22.

Osgood, Cornelius. *The Koreans and Their Culture.* New York: Ronald Press, 1951.

Peters, Richard, and Xiaobing Li. *Voices from the Korean War: Personal Stories of American, Korean, and Chinese Soldiers.* Lexington: University Press of Kentucky, 2004.

Pierpaoli, Paul G., Jr. "Beyond Collective Amnesia: A Korean War Retrospective." *International Social Science Review* 76, nos. 3–4 (2001): 92–102.

Popescu, Monica. "Translations: Lenin's Statues, Post-communism, and Post-apartheid." *Yale Journal of Criticism* 16, no. 2 (2003): 406–23.

Proisis, Theodore O. "The Collective Memory of the Atomic Bombings Misrecognized as Objective History: The Case of the Public Opposition to the National Air and Space Museum's Atom Bomb Exhibit." *Western Journal of Communication* 62, no. 3 (1998): 316–47.

Ritchin, Fred. *In Our Own Image: The Coming Revolution in Photography.* New York: Aperture Foundation, 1999.

Roberts, Richard C. "The Utah National Guard and Territorial Militias." In *Utah Historical Encyclopedia,* 596–98. Salt Lake City: University of Utah Press, 1994.

Roth, Mitchel P. *Historical Dictionary of War Journalism.* Westport, CT: Greenwood Press, 1997.

Roudometof, Victor. *Collective Memory, National Identity, and Ethnic Conflict: Greece, Bulgaria, and the Macedonian Question.* Westport, CT: Praeger, 2002.

Ruby, Jay. *Picturing Culture: Explorations of Film and Anthropology.* Chicago: University of Chicago Press, 2000.

Sabonis-Chafee, Theresa. "Communism as Kitsch: Soviet Symbols in Post-Soviet Society." In *Consuming Russia: Popular Culture, Sex, and Society Since Gorbachev,* edited by A. M. Barker, 362–81. Durham, NC: Duke University Press, 1999.

Saunders, Jack. "Records in the National Archives Relating to Korea, 1945–1950." In *Child of Conflict: The Korean-American Relationship, 1943–953,* edited by B. Cumings, 309–26. Seattle: University of Washington Press, 1983.

Saussure, Ferdinand de. "Nature of the Linguistic Sign and Immutability and Mutability of the Sign." In *Course in General Linguistics,* translated by W. Baskin, 65–78. 1915. Reprint, New York: McGraw-Hill, 1959.

Savage, Kirk. *Standing Soldiers, Kneeling Slaves: Race, War, and Monument in Nineteenth-Century America.* Princeton, NJ: Princeton University Press, 1997.

Schacter, Daniel L. *The Seven Sins of Memory: How the Mind Forgets and Remembers.* New York: Houghton Mifflin, 2001.

Schaller, Michael. *Douglas MacArthur: The Far Eastern General.* New York: Oxford University Press, 1989.

Scherer, Joanna C. "You Can't Believe Your Eyes: Inaccuracies in Photographs of North American Indians." *Studies in the Anthropology of Visual Communication* 2, no. 2 (1975): 67–95.

Schudson, Michael. "The Present in the Past Versus the Past in the Present." *Communication* 11, no. 2 (1989): 105–14.

———. *Watergate in American Memory: How We Remember, Forget, and Reconstruct the Past.* New York: Basic Books, 1992.

Schuman, Howard, and Jacqueline Scott. "Generations and Collective Memories." *American Sociological Review* 54 (1989): 359–81.

Schwartz, Barry. *Abraham Lincoln and the Forge of National Memory.* Chicago: University of Chicago Press, 2000.

———. "Frame Images: Towards a Semiotics of Collective Memory." *Semiotica* 121, nos. 1–2 (1998): 1–40.

———. "The Social Context of Commemoration: A Study in Collective Memory." *Social Forces* 6 (1982): 374–402.

Sen, Amartya. *Identity and Violence: The Illusion of Destiny.* New York: W. W. Norton, 2006.

Shopes, Linda. "Oral History and Community Involvement: The Baltimore Neighborhood Heritage Project." In *Presenting the Past: Essays on History and the Public,* edited by S. P. Benson, S. Brier, and R. Rosenzweig, 249–63. Philadelphia: Temple University, 1986.

Smith, Sidonie, and Julia Watson. *Reading Autobiography: A Guide for Interpreting Life Narratives.* Minneapolis: University of Minnesota Press, 2001.

Springer, Claudia. "Vietnam: A Television History and the Equivocal Nature of Objectivity." *Wide Angle* 7, no. 4 (1985): 53–60.

Stangl, Paul. "Revolutionaries' Cemeteries in Berlin: Memory, History, Place, and Space." *Urban History* 34, no. 3 (2007): 407–26.

Sturken, Marita. *Tangled Memories: The Vietnam War, the AIDS Epidemic, and the Politics of Remembering.* Berkeley: University of California Press, 1997.

Sturken, Marita, and Lisa Cartwright. *Practices of Looking: An Introduction to Visual Culture.* Oxford, UK: Oxford University Press, 2001.

Thompson, Paul. *The Voice of the Past: Oral History.* 3rd ed. New York: Oxford University Press, 2000.

Till, Karen E. *The New Berlin: Memory, Politics, Place.* Minneapolis: University of Minnesota Press, 2005.

Toplin, Robert Brent. "The Filmmaker as Historian." *American Historical Review* 93, no. 5 (1988): 1210–27.

Tumarkin, Nina. *Lenin Lives! The Lenin Cult in Soviet Russia.* Cambridge, MA: Harvard University Press, 1983.

———. *The Living and the Dead: The Rise and Fall of the Cult of World War II in Russia.* New York: Basic Books, 1994.

Urrutia, Benjamin. "The Korean War and Utah." In *Utah Historical Encyclopedia,* edited by A. Powell, 306–7. Salt Lake City: University of Utah, 1994.

Verdery, Katherine. *The Political Lives of Dead Bodies: Reburial and Postsocialist Change.* New York: Columbia University Press, 1999.

Wagstaff, Jeremy. "Korea's New Crusaders." *Far Eastern Economic Review* 167, no. 40 (2004): 32–34.

Weathersby, Kathryn. "The Soviet Role in the Early Phase of the Korean War: New Documentary Evidence." *Journal of American-East Asian Relations* 2, no. 4 (1993): 425–58.

Williams, Terry T. *Refugee: An Unnatural History of Family and Place.* New York: Vintage Books, 2001.

Winter, Jay. *Remembering War: The Great War Between Memory and History in the Twentieth Century.* New Haven, CT: Yale University Press, 2006.

Yampolsky, Mikhail. "In the Shadow of Monuments: Notes on Iconoclasm and Time." In *Soviet Hieroglyphics: Visual Culture in Late Twentieth Century Russia,* edited by N. Condee, translated by J. Kachur, 93–112. Bloomington: Indiana University Press, 1995.

Yoneyama, Lisa. "For Transformative Knowledge and Postnationalist Public Sphere: The Smithsonian *Enola Gay* Controversy." In *Perilous Memories: The Asia-Pacific War(s),* edited by F. G. White and L. Yoneyama, 323–46. Durham, NC: Duke University Press, 2001.

Young, James E. "Between History and Memory: The Voice of the Eyewitness." In *Witness and Memory,* edited by A. Douglass and T. A. Vogler. New York: Routledge, 2003.

———. "The Counter-monument: Memory Against Itself in Germany Today." *Critical Inquiry* 18, no. 2 (1992): 267–96.

———. *The Texture of Memory: Holocaust Memorials and Meaning.* New Haven, CT: Yale University Press, 1993.

Zelizer, Barbie. "Reading the Past Against the Grain: The Shape of Memory Studies." *Critical Studies in Mass Communication* 12, no. 2 (1995): 214–39.

———. *Remembering to Forget: Holocaust Memory Through the Camera's Eye.* Chicago: University of Chicago Press, 1998.

INDEX

Page numbers in italics refer to illustrations.

female researchers, war survivor attitudes toward, 32

fiftieth anniversary of Korean War: commemoration, 74, 80, 81, 83; counter-memories in context of, 5; documentaries at time of, 56; memorials built in time for, 73; memories heightened during, 1–2; memory construction in context of, 115, 116–17

filial piety, 41, 43

forgetting: Korean War shaped by act of, 13; memorials promoting, 94; memory selection role of, 28; willful, impact of, 13

forgotten war: explanation of, 74; term, 82; view contested, 92

Forgotten War, The (documentary film), 56

Freedom Park (South Korea), 96, 102, *104*, 105, 108, 109, *109*

gender roles, 41

Goffman, Erving, 10

good war (mythical narrative), 73–74, 79, 87–92, 93

Great Man theory of history, 67

guerrilla warfare, 68

Gulf War, 63

Halbwachs, Maurice, 75, 98

Hanley, Charles, 9

hegemony: challenges to, 76, 97, 101, 107, 109–10, 111, 113; defined, 12; forgetting role in, 13; memorials and monuments, 96; narrative and, xi, 13, 17, 29, 115; statue role in, 5, 98, 101, 107, 109

Henke, Suzette, 45, 46

heroic figures, 61–62, 90

hero-oriented readings of war, 51

Herschaft, Randy, 9

Higgins, Margaret, 16

Hill Air Force Museum, 118

historical documentaries: ambiguity, building in, 65; epistemological aspect of, 59, 64; limitations of, 70; visual archives and, 61, 64

historical events, anniversaries of, 1

historical narratives, reconstruction of, 96

historical sites, 98

Holocaust, commemoration of, 99

human life span, limited, memory endurance deterred by, 98

iconoclasm, 108–12

Ill-equipped troops' unfortunate mistake (media theme), 15–17, 23

image: heroic figure images, 61, 62; as representational tool, 59; syntax of, 58. *See also terms starting with* visual

image events, 101

Im Ke Ri, refugees from, 19, 20

immortality, statues conveying impression of, 98–99

Incheon Landing, 62, 96, 97, 102, 103, 105

individual memory, collective memory relationship to, 75, 76, 79, 93

internal warfare (Korea), 68

international context of Korean War: archival films and, 61; counter-narratives and, 46; multiple narratives, 6; power relations, international as war factor, 13

"interviewer/interviewee" (term), 11

Iraq war, 69, 83

I Remember Korea, 14

Japanese colonialism: aftermath and legacy of, 14, 66; as communism development factor, 26; counter-memories illuminating, 55; as Korean War factor, 13, 67; land dispossession under, 67; legacy of, 78

Jayu Park (South Korea). *See* Freedom Park (South Korea)

Kang, Jeong-Koo, 106

Keum, Cho-Ja: injuries suffered by, 33, 36, 37; language background of, 22–23; mother recalled by, 36–37

and, 70–71; images studied by, 58; memory construction site linkage as goal of, 28–29; memory reconstruction explored by, 2

memory sites, 115

memory studies, 2–3, 5–6

memory texts, volume of, 92

Mendoza, Martha, 9

mental healing, 45

military conscription, 41

military tactics, 57, 59, 63

mnemonic objects, 95–96, 99

monarchical government, 41

monuments. *See* memorials and monuments; statues; *and name of memorial, e.g.:* Korean War Veterans Memorial

Mormon pioneers, 79–80

motherhood: Confucian script of, 3, 32, 33, 42–43, 44, 45, 51, 116; No Gun Ri survivor attitudes concerning, 33–38; as rhetorical device, 43–45, 49; script of, 50; sons, importance to mother's identity, 41; unspeakable memories, scripting with, 40–43, 44–45, 51

My Lai massacre (1969), 9

mythical narrative: collective-individual memory relationship and, 76; veterans, impact on, 93; war memorials resonating with, 79

napalm girl (Vietnam), 64

narratives: construction, image fragility in, 58; hegemony, competition for, xi; limitations of, 58; mythical, 76, 79, 93; themes, common in, 15

narrativizing, 12–13, 16

"narrator" (term), 11

nation, constructed and incomplete nature of, 112–13

natural disasters, 80, 83

new-media technology, 97

No Gun Ri Bridge, *8,* 12, 30

No Gun Ri Committee, 50

No Gun Ri killings: investigation of, 9–10, 12; Korean media review of, 107; memorial ceremonies, 30, *31,* 45; survivor narratives (female), xi, 2, 3, 22, 31–52, 116; survivor narratives (general), 8–9, 11, 12, 19–29, 115–16; survivors in United States, 48–49; U.S. government position on, 10

No Gun Ri killings, U.S. media coverage of: in Cold War era, 25; common themes, 15–19, 23; communism subject treatment in, 26; counter-voices, 10–11; impact of, 9–10; journalists' eyewitness accounts, 22; as memory site, xi, 2; North Korean soldier stories missing from, 24; overview of, 7–8; post–Cold War, 14; remembering and forgetting, 3; survivor testimonies differing from, 21, 24, 25, 115–16; survivor testimonies used in, 8, 20, 30

nonverbal expression, 47–48, 51–52

North, Michael, 112

North Korea: nuclear testing, 117; Soviet control of, 69; starvation in, 88; traumatic memories, 117–18; UN forces in, 62; U.S. relationship with, 65–66

North Korean officers, writings of, 55

North Korean soldiers: images of, 25; refugees saved by, 21, 24, 25

official narrative of Korean War: anniversaries and commemoration, 74; collective amnesia role in maintaining, 53; countering, 4, 101, 107, 110, 113–14, 115; documentary films reinforcing, 57, 60, 70–71, 116; MacArthur and, 96; media role in maintaining, 116; memorials reflecting, 54; veterans' memories at odds with (*see* veterans: memories, personal versus official narratives); war literature constructed from, 55

On Collective Memory (Halbwachs), 75

oral history interview techniques, 11, 32

orality, exorcising inarticulable memories with, 45–52

oral testimonies, devaluation of, 26

Osborne, John, 23

Osgood, Cornelius, 18, 26

Park, Sun-Yong: children's deaths recalled by, 37–38, 44–45; No Gun Ri killings recalled by, 22, 33, 46, 50; son, effort to protect, 43

past events, transformation of, 12

past relationship to present: documentary film treatment of, 65–66; memory construction and, 118; soldiers' witnessing and, 77; understanding, 5

perceived events, past events transformed into, 12

Peterson, Clarence, 90

Pierpaoli, Paul, 14, 54

"police action" (term), 77

political ideology fears, self-censorship due to, 8, 25

popular culture, 54, 90

post-traumatic stress disorder, 40

prisoners of war, 90–91

protected zone, myth of, 51

Public Broadcasting Service (PBS), 56–57, 66–67

public opinion on Korean War, 77–78

public space, politicizing, 100

racial tensions, 21–22, 23

Reaveley, Don, 82, 86–87

refugees: at No Gun Ri, 19; U.S. military attacks on, 10–11, 18, 19, 21

"regret" (term), 10

Remembering War (Winter), 76

"researcher" (term), 11

resilience (mythical narrative), 73–74, 79–83, 92

resistance groups, 66

Rhee, Syngman, 102, 105

Russian officers, writings of, 55

Salvation by hospitable Communists (survivors' theme), 15, 23–26

Schaller, Michael, 107

scholars, Korean War unpopular with, 54

Schuman, Howard, 54–55

Scott, Jacqueline, 55

"scriptotherapy" (term), 45, 49

sculpture, vanishing forms of, 99

self-censorship, 8, 25

Sen, Amartya, 78

shamanism, 104, 105

Smith, Sidonie, 33

social class, 68

soldiers, South Korean, 107

soldiers, U.S. *See* U.S. soldiers/military

sons (in Korean culture): importance of, 41; protection and sacrifices for, 43

sounds of images, 59–60

South Korea: postwar conditions, 91, 106–7; subversive war accounts spread in, 107; United States, relationship with, 105, 117; U.S. occupation of, 69

South Korean police: at MacArthur statue protests, 105, 106, 110, 111; before and during war, 111; wartime atrocities, 13

South Korean troops, civilians killed by, 107

Soviet archives, declassification of, 55

Soviet bloc, former: archives released from, 14; statues in, 95, 105, 108

Soviet Union: dissolution of, 96; in Korean Peninsula, 14, 69

space-time relationship, 113

Stalin, Joseph V., 61, 67, 95

state, obedience to, 43

statues: Communist, collapse of, 108; conflicting meanings of, 101; disposal of, 95; as dissenting medium, 97–98, 115, 116; in Korea, 103–5; rhetoric, contextualizing, 98–101; Soviet, 95, 105, 108; transformation of, 95, 97, 101

stories, (de)selection of, 5

androcentric discourse of, 42, 50, 51, 52; media coverage of, 69–70

war dead: honoring, 80; names, inscribing, 84, *85*, 85–87

War in Korea (Higgins), 16

war memorials: building, 73, 92; commemorative sites, delay in establishing, 79; meanings of, 74; message conveyed by, 93; World War II and Korean War joint, 87. *See also specific memorial, e.g.:* Utah Korean War Memorial

war memories, role in forging national myths, narratives, and identities, 76

Watson, Julie, 33

We Can Talk Now (TV series), 107

white clothing, U.S. military attitude toward people in, 18

Winter, Jay, 76

women: Confucian norms, 41–43; in war, 38–39, 42

World Trade Organization Conference (Seattle, 1999), 110

World War I, 80, 81, 83

World War II: Korean War associated with, 87–88, 93; memorials, 76, 81, 83, 87; myths from, 87; statues, 96; veterans, 76

wounds, exposing, 48

written narrative, 45–46, 47

Yang, Hae-Suk: eye loss suffered by, 35, 48, 49; mother recalled by, 35–36, 43; No Gun Ri killings recalled by, 33; North Korean soldiers recalled by, 24, 25; trip to United States by, 48

Yeosu, revolt of, 68

Young, James, 99

young males, escape from No Gun Ri, 39, 46